DAVID LODGE

David Lodge (CBE)'s novels include *Changing Places*, *Small World* and *Nice Work* (shortlisted for the Booker) and, most recently, *A Man of Parts*. He has also written plays and screenplays, and several books of literary criticism. His works have been translated into more than thirty languages. His previous volumes of memoir are *Quite a Good Time to be Born* and *Writer's Luck*.

He is Emeritus Professor of English Literature at the University of Birmingham, a Fellow of the Royal Society of Literature, and is a Chevalier de l'Ordre des Arts et des Lettres.

ALSO BY DAVID LODGE

Fiction

Criticism

Essays

Drama

Memoirs

DAVID LODGE

Varying Degrees of Success

A Memoir: 1992–2020

VINTAGE

1 3 5 7 9 10 8 6 4 2

Vintage is part of the Penguin Random House group of companies
whose addresses can be found at global.penguinrandomhouse.com

Penguin
Random House
UK

Copyright © David Lodge 2021

David Lodge has asserted his right to be identified as the author of this
Work in accordance with the Copyright, Designs and Patents Act 1988

First published in Vintage in 2022
First published in hardback by Harvill Secker in 2021

penguin.co.uk/vintage

A CIP catalogue record for this book is available from the British Library

ISBN 9781529114898

Printed and bound in Great Britain by Clays Ltd, Elcograf S.p.A.

The authorised representative in the EEA is Penguin Random House Ireland,
Morrison Chambers, 32 Nassau Street, Dublin D02 YH68

Penguin Random House is committed to a sustainable future
for our business, our readers and our planet. This book is made
from Forest Stewardship Council® certified paper.

To Mary, once again, for her help and encouragement.

FOREWORD

The words 'success' and 'succeed' appear quite frequently in the pages of my memoirs, and certainly in this volume, usually measured in terms of sales, audience figures, reviews, literary prizes and awards. I'm aware that this may seem boastful and mercenary, but there is no other honest way to describe the motivation and introspection of a professional writer. It is rare for anyone to write a novel or a play exclusively for their own enjoyment. A novel invites and requires a reader to respond to it. The author writes with the intention of attracting and holding the readers' attention – moving them, making them laugh, making them think. The same applies to plays in live theatre, with the important difference that the audience is physically present to manifest their enjoyment, or the lack of it.

Writing for publication or performance in any form is a gratuitous act – a choice, not an obligation – and only some degree of success will seem to justify the effort required to perform it. Hence the tension and anxiety which often trouble an author as the date of publication or first night approaches, and he or she waits to see the first reviews. Prose fiction and drama are competitive fields of endeavour, and the first of these has been made even more so by the proliferation of prizes like the Booker and its many imitators which, with the eager co-operation of the media, have made competition between writers explicit. Poetry, playwriting and screenplay writing have similar exposure to the lottery of awards funded by sponsors and institutions for their own publicity purposes. Authors cannot remain indifferent to such indications of how their work is being received, though they rarely speak or write openly about them.

As my intention in writing my memoirs was to give a candid and comprehensive account of one writer's life, I have described my experience of successful and disappointing outcomes in my professional career, with explicit reference to positive and negative reviews, sales figures, the reception of books in foreign countries, the length of time they remain in print, and other such objective indicators, in the belief that my readers will find this information of interest. I am encouraged by the fact that the word 'honest' occurs quite often in letters from readers writing to express their appreciation.

Both 'success' and 'failure' are imprecise concepts which different people will apply differently to works of art according to their predilections and prejudices. There are many possible degrees of success, as the title I have given to this memoir is meant to convey, but the book is not just about that. It is also about my personal life, my family, friends, colleagues and collaborators, and the travels to other countries that I was fortunately invited to undertake as a result of my work as a writer. With its two predecessors, it amounts to a fairly comprehensive autobiography.

D.L., January 2021

1

The two preceding volumes of my memoirs differed from each other in scope and scale. The first, *Quite a Good Time to Be Born*,[1] covered my life from birth in 1935 to the age of forty, and described how I became a writer, principally of prose fiction and literary criticism, beginning with the early experiences and influences that fed into my work later. It concluded with the publication of my first really successful novel, *Changing Places*, in 1975. The second volume, *Writer's Luck*, published in 2018, tracked my life in greater detail over a shorter period, 1976–91, which was a particularly fertile and prosperous one for literary fiction in Britain, and for me personally. In 1986 I retired early from the academic career which I had previously combined with creative writing, to become a full-time freelance author. I continued to write and publish literary criticism, but it was directed at an audience outside as well as inside the groves of academe, mainly in collections of essays and reviews, and in a book called *The Art of Fiction* published in

---

[1] Henceforth this book is referred to as QAGTTBB.

1991, based on a series of weekly articles in the *Independent on Sunday* newspaper.

I have always seized opportunities to try my hand in various genres and different media, a trait I see as replicating my father's versatility as musician, singer and actor. It was also encouraged by the example of Malcolm Bradbury, my friend and colleague at the University of Birmingham in the 1960s, who had been writing humorous pieces for *Punch* and comedy scripts for radio as well as fiction and literary criticism before I met him. I described in *QAGTTBB* how in 1963 Malcolm persuaded the Artistic Director of the Birmingham Rep to commission and produce a satirical revue written by the two of us and a gifted postgraduate student, Jim Duckett. It was my first experience of working with professional actors speaking my lines, in rehearsal and in public performance, and I found it fascinating. It left me predisposed to one day attempt a full-length play, when an appropriate idea presented itself – as it did in 1985. After many drafts and several efforts to mount a production, this play, called *The Writing Game*, was premiered at the Birmingham Rep in May, 1990, and had a long and varied life subsequently.

Between the 1960s and the 1990s television rapidly developed as a medium for drama, and Malcolm was again ahead of me in writing a TV play, in collaboration with Christopher Bigsby, called *The After Dinner Game*, produced at the BBC's Birmingham Pebble Mill studios in 1975, though he had moved to the University of East Anglia by then, and lived in Norwich. There he became a prolific writer of TV screenplays, both original and adapted. I made several efforts to emulate him, and succeeded with the adaptation of my own novel, *Nice Work*, for the BBC in 1969. The dramatic strand in my writing career extended into the period covered by the present volume in the form of two new stage plays, *Home Truths* and *Secret Thoughts*, and several commissioned screenplays for television drama and feature films – all adaptations of novels, some of them my own. Most of these scripts went through several drafts but were not produced, with the exception of my adaptation of Charles Dickens' *Martin Chuzzlewit* for the BBC, broadcast in 1994.

This kind of work was always interesting even when it was frustrating, but the novel remained the form to which I was most committed. As a novelist you are the moral owner of the work and wholly in control of it. The collaborative dimension of theatre, feature films and TV drama is stimulating, but it sometimes requires you to accept advice that you don't really believe in, as the price of seeing the project through to completion. Of course, it can happen that a publisher will reject your latest novel when you submit it, or demand revisions which you cannot accept (which happened to me early in my career with *Changing Places*, as described in *QAGTTBB*). But if you have developed a good relationship with your editor and with the executive head of the firm, as I had with Secker & Warburg, that is an unlikely outcome.

The good relationship depends upon a degree of consistency and continuity in the work you produce. For that reason most novelists have a dread of one day running out of inspiration, and like to have a provisional idea for their next novel while they are seeing their latest one into print. On the 21st of September 1991, the month in which *Paradise News* was published, I started a loose-leaf notebook which eventually took up most of the space in a standard size A4 ring binder. The first entry reads as follows:

Vague idea stirring for novel no.10. About a man who lives in Rummidge but has reasons to go to London frequently, and rents or buys a flat near Leicester Square. The novel to turn on the contrast between the two cities. Possible title: *Intercity*.

Any reader of *Writer's Luck* would identify the source of this idea as my purchase of a small flat near Leicester Square as a *pied à terre* in 1991. But the contrast between London and Birmingham was a minor theme in the novel that grew from this seed, and although it contains some satirical commentary on the deficiencies and discomforts of the rail service between those cities in the last years of British Rail, it was not called *Intercity*. It was called *Therapy*.

In the second half of 1991 I was undergoing physiotherapy for an occasional excruciating pain in the right knee, and eventually accepted a consultant's opinion that I needed an operation called an arthroscopy to clean up the joint. For some time I had been seeking help from a counsellor for anxiety and depression, and more recently from a clinical psychologist who practised Cognitive Behavioural Therapy, then a relatively new form of treatment. I also became the patient of a colleague at Birmingham University who had retired from academic life and was pursuing a new career as an acupuncturist. I was always calmer after these sessions, and although they had no long-lasting effect, I felt I was acting positively instead of doing nothing. The increasing popularity of all sorts of therapies from aromatherapy to reflexology was a distinctive feature of the last decade of the twentieth century. The sixties had been about Politics, the seventies had been about Sex, the eighties had been about Money, and the nineties were about Therapy. I believed I had a timely subject for a novel, and relevant personal experience to draw on. There is a significant entry in the notebook some time after the first one:

> I have had a new idea for this novel . . . to make it more personal and autobiographical, exploring, in a comic mode as far as possible, a neurosis of my own which I have been struggling with for some years now, and have never really dealt with in fiction, namely my tendency to get into states of depression and anxiety, especially where decisions are concerned, either being unable to make up my mind or regretting a decision once it is irrevocable – only to change my mind again when it is realised.

Gradually, tentatively, I developed elements of the novel in the notebook. For some time I referred to the main character as 'Z', but eventually I gave him a name, Laurence ('Tubby') Passmore, and an occupation: writer of a very popular TV sitcom, which would require him to travel frequently between Rummidge (my fictional version of Birmingham in previous novels) and London. He would occupy a comfortable house in a leafy outer suburb of Rummidge, with an attractive, sexy wife called Sally absorbed in her own career in higher education, and have a platonic relationship with a casting director called Amy in London. But I had no idea at that stage of what would happen to him and the other characters.

At this time I was vacillating over the purchase of a new car. I was attracted to the Mazda 626, a sleek, seductive vehicle, but I brooded and procrastinated, thinking it was unpatriotic to buy a Japanese car, and risky to put myself in the hands of a small British dealership. Eventually I bought the Mazda, and was delighted with it. But it was not only decision-making that worried me. I felt that I was not enjoying my life as much as I should, given that I was well off and professionally successful. The knee problem was especially lowering to my spirits, and I looked forward hopefully to the surgical solution. I had heard of young tennis players who were back on court a few weeks after the operation, but that was not the outcome in my case. I spent some time confined to the house with my swollen leg supported on a pouf, and after that I was obliged to get about with the aid of a stick for a couple of months. By following the prescribed physiotherapy exercises religiously, I gradually became more mobile and able to pick up the threads of my professional life.

There was still no prospect of a London production of *The Writing Game*, but the Manchester Library Theatre, second in status in that city, put on a production in March and I went up there to attend some rehearsals and several performances. The director of the theatre and of my play was Chris Honer, a quietly spoken and level-headed man who had been attracted to the play because he liked my novels, and we got on well. The theatre's budget meant that the cast was below that of the Rep production in experience and reputation, but they were adequate, and I thought the actor who played Leo was often better than Lou Hirsch in this role. The main problem was that the actress who played Maude lacked self-confidence – exactly what the character has in spades. I wrote in my diary: 'I suppose I have become an excessively critical member of an audience for this play. I am like the conductor of a piece of music which he knows backwards, alert to every slight fault or hesitation in the performance.' I wondered if perhaps I was finally coming to the end of my interest in *The Writing Game*, but it was revived by the news that an American producer called Jack Temchin, who had seen the play at the American Repertory Theatre in Cambridge Mass., was negotiating an option to produce it in New York off-Broadway.

In April 1992 I went to America to do a five-city book tour with *Paradise News*, starting in Los Angeles, where I met Michael Bloom, Jack Temchin's choice of director for his prospective production of *The Writing Game*, and finishing in New York, where I met Jack himself. He turned out to be a small, thin, shrewd Jewish American of Polish origin, with a quick ironic wit, and we got on together straight away. That evening Jack accompanied me to Books and Company, a shop on Madison Avenue where I gave a reading, an event later amusingly memorialised in a personal small ad at the back of the *New York Review of Books*:

> *Books & Co 4/13 – you told David Lodge you were touched by the romance in* Paradise News. *Later, we crossed paths on stairs (I am slim brunette SWF). I would like to talk with you. So slim the possibility of your seeing this, I am encouraging other Lodge enthusiasts to respond.*

I hoped they did, and perhaps formed a book circle dedicated to my novels.

News of Jack Temchin's project reached me intermittently in the remainder of 1992 and beyond, as various proposals for casting, and for provincial theatres where the play might be launched preparatory to opening it in New York, were tabled and cancelled with monotonous regularity. Fortunately, I received an intriguing proposition which promised a real break from the tedium of this waiting game, and an enticing change of scene. A producer/director in the Religious Department of BBC television, David Willcock, called me one day to say that they were going to make three one-hour TV films about historic religious pilgrimages, written and presented by well-known writers, beginning with the pilgrimage to Santiago de Compostela in Galicia, north-west Spain, and he wanted me to write and present it. That I was a Roman Catholic and had written about that faith had been a factor in his choice. The filming would start in late June, following one of the traditional routes, from Le Puy in south-east France to the shrine of St James the Apostle in Santiago a thousand miles away to the west, travelling by car, stopping occasionally to film at places of interest, and finishing with the Santiago fiesta in the last week of July. I accepted the invitation readily because I was interested in the concept of pilgrimage and its secularisation in modern tourism, and had made some play with this theme in *Paradise News*; also because it promised to be a kind of working holiday, just the thing to lift my spirits after the lowering winter months.

The team consisted of David himself, a cameraman, a sound man, their respective assistants, and myself. The cameraman was Bill Megalos, an energetic American from California, who specialised in documentary filmmaking and was very good at it. He had brought his mountain bike with him and at the end of the day's work liked to set off into the locality, wherever it was, for a spin.

We had three cars, one of them mainly for my exclusive use. It was a brand new Renault cabriolet, dark red with cream leather upholstery, which attracted many admiring and envious glances along the way. I had never driven a convertible with the top down before, and I enjoyed it enormously, since the weather was perfect for the experience. Like all such documentaries, the film pretended I was a lone pilgrim, but we were not going to disguise the fact that I was making the pilgrimage the easy way – rather, it was foregrounded as a kind of running joke. My progress across France was recorded in shots of me driving the Renault along country roads against scenic and picturesque backgrounds. Medieval pilgrims received a plenary indulgence (i.e. divine forgiveness for all their sins to date) when they reached Santiago. Modern pilgrims could get a certificate, known as a 'compostela', on arrival if they possessed a kind of passport stamped at various points along the Camino to prove that they had walked at least part of the way. The film would end with me trying and failing to get my compostela from a suspicious priest.

The pilgrimage was enormously popular in the Middle Ages, and literally millions of people, like Chaucer's Wife of Bath in the prologue of *The Canterbury Tales*, made it on horseback or on foot. From the sixteenth century onwards it fell into gradual decline, but it was revived in modern times by an alliance between the Catholic Church and the Spanish tourist industry, and has thrived. In fact it has recently become, like so many 'heritage' attractions, too popular in some respects to be comfortably enjoyed, and we were fortunate to film the journey when we did. The full experience really begins at the little town of St-Jean-Pied-de-Port in Gascony, where the traditional pilgrimage routes through France converge at the foot of a pass over the Pyrenees, after which there is only one route – the Camino. Here we stayed for a few days in a Michelin-approved hotel which was a welcome change from the one-star accommodation we had on the road. I was kitted out with a rucksack and a staff to give me the semblance of being a pilgrim when I was filmed walking, though the rucksack was lightly packed and the rest of my belongings travelled behind me by car.

In the morning of the 3rd of July, a fine day, I set off to climb the winding road that leads to the summit of the pass, Bill Megalos preceding me with his camera. The higher we walked, the more splendid were the views. David had spotted a middle-aged couple coming up behind us, and persuaded them to engage me in conversation as we walked together, so they had to endure my fractured French for a while. They were devout Catholics, and had walked all the way from Le Puy. At the top of the pass I met Nico, a Dutch artist with no religious faith who had walked all the way from Rotterdam, and was aiming to get to Santiago to celebrate his fortieth birthday. Modern pilgrims on the Camino have all kinds of motives: religious, personal, cultural, recreational. For some it is a profound rite of passage, for others a holiday with a difference.

On the other side of the pass the road descends to the Augustinian abbey of Roncesvalles, a name that vibrates with historical and literary associations, such as Charlemagne and *The Song of Roland*, which in the heyday of the pilgrimage gave pilgrims free meals and lodging for three days. Modern pilgrims stay for one night and pay a reasonable fee. Even the most secular of them seem sensitive to the atmosphere of religious spirituality in this place, and most attend the mass which is celebrated in the abbey church every evening.

Our next stop was Pamplona, an abrupt change of ambience. The fiesta of Saint Fermin was in progress, an event more pagan than Christian in character, famous for the running of bulls through the narrow streets of the old town on their way to the bull ring, goaded by young men running beside them, eager to display their machismo. The next morning's newspaper reported how many had been gored, or otherwise injured. David had booked a room with a balcony overlooking the bull run to film the spectacle, so we had a good view, but bull-fighting and its associated rituals is an element of Spanish culture which I find wholly alien and I did not enjoy it.

Next day we were back on the Camino, stopping occasionally to film me walking a short distance with my rucksack and staff, sometimes in the wrong direction because the light was better for filming. Two historic cities lay ahead, Burgos and Leon, both boasting exceptionally fine Gothic cathedrals, and between them lies the Meseta, a vast empty plain that must be as testing to the spirit as to the stamina of a solitary pilgrim walking, or even cycling across it. Increasing numbers choose the latter mode of transport, and are somewhat looked down on by the hikers. The further we progressed on the Camino, the more pilgrims we overtook, in ones, pairs and groups, on foot or on bikes. All along the route there are hostels called *refugios* where by tradition pilgrims are offered free overnight shelter. They vary in character from barns with earth floors on which the pilgrims spread their sleeping bags, to renovated old buildings with mod cons like showers and proper beds. David had booked us into one of the latter type, which was efficiently managed by a volunteer English couple. There was a spacious unisex dormitory on the first floor with rows of bunk beds mostly occupied that night by a Catholic youth group. They were obviously enjoying themselves, but prepared decorously for sleep. By arrangement I was woken at 6 a.m. by the crew and had to simulate surprise and dismay at this early start for the camera.

About halfway through the shooting schedule a one-week break had been inserted for some members of the team, including myself, to rejoin their families and take care of business. In the days prior to this interval I was solicited by the two production assistants, Kate Johnson and Linda Flanigan, supported by Bill Megalos, to cooperate in playing a practical joke on David. He was a wonderfully efficient producer, but like most perfectionists somewhat domineering, and they wanted to take him down a peg or two. I was to send a hoax message from England that I was prevented from returning to Spain as scheduled for an indefinite length of time, which I was to communicate just before we were due to resume filming. If that actually happened it would be a catastrophe for the production, and I was reluctant to agree, but eventually I was persuaded. After all, they said, it would only cause David anxiety for a very short time before I turned up at Valladolid airport where he was scheduled to meet me, and they intimated that this kind of ragging was not uncommon during extensive filming away from home. There was also a subtext in my own thoughts which nudged me towards agreement. David had conveyed to me some time earlier that the team had complained to him that I was failing to project sufficient enthusiasm as presenter in the film, and he shared their opinion. They also resented my tendency to sit down and read a book when nothing much else was happening, instead of chatting with them. I thought I might redeem myself in their eyes by collaborating in the hoax. I didn't commit myself, but said I would think about it when I got home.

It didn't take me long to devise a plot. About a week earlier our caravan of cars had been caught in a traffic violation by the *Policia* on the open road. It involved an unexpected diversion and an illegal turn at the approach to a bridge, and a posse of policemen was waiting to halt our progress and impose fines. We had the impression that this was not an uncommon event. The senior officer, who spoke some English, identified David as the leader of our little convoy, spoke sternly to him about the seriousness of the offence, examined our passports and wrote down our names and other details in his notebook. David pleaded unfamiliarity with Spanish road signs and after a long discussion, at the end of which some banknotes changed hands, we were allowed to proceed. This episode inspired my hoax. I knew the address of the hotel where David and the rest of the team were staying, and two days before I was due to return I airmailed a letter to say I had been informed by the Spanish Embassy that I was implicated in a serious traffic violation case in Spain and had left the country without paying the appropriate fine, and in consequence I would not be allowed to re-enter it. I calculated that by the time David received this message, I would have left Birmingham on my way back to Spain via my London flat and he wouldn't be able to reach me. Recalling Malcolm's article in the *Observer* on the 1st of April 1984,[2] which fooled many readers, about a newly discovered French genius called Henri Mensonge who had anticipated all the key ideas of structuralism and poststructuralism years before Barthes, Derrida and Co., I instructed David, if he wanted further information, to call a London telephone number (belonging to a Spanish restaurant chosen at random) and ask to speak to Señor Mentira, a name which, like 'Mensonge' means 'lie'.

David was waiting to meet me at Valladolid airport with a countenance which as I approached him gave nothing away. 'So you managed to get through Immigration,' he said, ironically rather than with relief, for he had guessed by this time that he had been hoaxed. But the others in the conspiracy told me later that on receipt of my letter he had been seriously panicked, because the connection with the *Policia* episode made it so plausible. He took the jape in good part however, and it did not affect our relationship.

A few days later our caravan crossed from Castile into Galicia, a large chunk of north-west Spain, of which Santiago is the principal city. It is a terrain of outstanding natural beauty, consisting mainly of green hills, some the size of small mountains, and a spectacular coastline. The culture is agrarian and reputed to be matriarchal, though some anthropologists are sceptical. I did however observe a peasant woman of formidable build and stern features barking instructions to a dispirited-looking man bent over some agricultural task, which seemed to support the matriarchy theory. At this time we were

[2] See *Writer's Luck* pp. 194–5.

staying at a *refugio* in Cebreiro, a village that sits on top of a steep hill above the Camino which is a shrine in its own right, being the site of a medieval miracle story about a lazy and sceptical priest who was shocked back into fervent faith by the transformation of the Eucharistic bread and wine into real flesh and blood. The original chalice and paten are displayed in the chapel.

The *refugio*'s accommodation was rather basic, being little more than a couple of barns with bedsteads and blankets, but it had a canteen serving good food. There I had an unexpected encounter with another writer. I was having lunch with the team when a dark-haired young man entered and sat down at the end of the refectory table where we were seated. He quickly discovered what we were doing in this place and revealed that he was writing about the pilgrimage himself, for inclusion in a book about Catholic Europe. We chatted for a while and then he suddenly asked me a question which had nothing to do with the Camino: 'What did Chad's family make their fortune from in *The Ambassadors*?' he asked. 'No one knows,' I replied. 'But there's a solution in your first novel,' he said. 'My third novel,' I corrected him. 'You're David Lodge,' he said, and I confirmed that I was. The young man introduced himself as Colm Tóibín, whom I knew to be an Irish novelist and non-fiction writer, though I was not familiar with his work. He appeared to know mine very well, however. The riddle he put to me and its solution occur in my novel *The British Museum is Falling Down*, (actually my third one, published in 1965). The hero's best friend, Camel, like himself a postgraduate student doing research in the British Museum, is writing a doctoral thesis on 'Sanitation in Victorian Fiction' and speculates that the 'unnamed, small, trivial, rather ridiculous object of the commonest use', on the manufacture of which the Newsome family fortune in Henry James' *The Ambassadors* is based, and which is never named in the novel, is a chamber pot. That Colm Tóibín should choose to identify me in this challenging way on the first occasion we met, alluding to a crux in the work of Henry James, seemed eerily prophetic in retrospect in 2004 when we both

15

published biographical novels about James. That coincidence will be described in its place later in this volume, and readers who wish to read the full story in detail will find it in my book *The Year of Henry James, or Timing Is All: the Story of a Novel*, published two years later. But I have a postscript to add here. On the 10th of February 2010, I made the following entry in my diary: 'Looking in Somerset Maugham's book, *The Vagrant Mood: Six Essays* (1952) for information about H.G. Wells, I came across this passage about Henry James in the essay, 'Some Novelists I have Known':

> I am not sure that Henry James was fortunate in his friends . . . The reverence with which they treated him was of no great service to him. They seemed to me, indeed, a trifle silly: they whispered to one another with delighted giggles that Henry James privately stated that the article in *The Ambassadors* on the manufacture of which the fortune of the widow Newsome was founded, and the nature of which he had left in polite obscurity, was in fact a chamber pot.

I was astonished and delighted to discover that the solution to the identity of the 'commonest object', which I thought I had invented, and attributed to one of my fictional characters, was actually true.

When Colm's book on Catholic Europe was published, I reviewed it and read his description of our lunchtime meeting in Cebreiro with particular interest. He had been travelling alone, evidently feeling lonely, and envied our group, which he would have liked to join. 'The crew was full of jokes and nicknames for each other, completely bonded as a group,' he wrote. 'They even called David Lodge "Lodgie".' I was pleased by his impression of a happy united team. I thought that the hoax episode might have had the effect I had hoped for; but perhaps it was just the shared knowledge that after so many days on the road we were approaching the goal of our journey.

*

The last stop on the Camino before Santiago itself is the village of Labacolla, traditionally the place where pilgrims wash themselves and their clothes before entering the city. I had talked to David about possibly walking the last stage on my own for a change, and the next morning I was filmed setting off and waving goodbye to the rest of the team. I took a pocket dictaphone with me to record my thoughts, fancying that being alone I might feel some spiritual dimension to the pilgrimage that had escaped me when making the film. It didn't happen. The beginning of the route was a pleasant stroll through woods, but my first sight of the distant cathedral with its three spires from the 'Hill of Joy' on the outskirts of the city was spoiled by a huge excavation in progress. An amphitheatre was being built in preparation for a surge in the number of pilgrims expected the following year, designated a 'Holy Year'. From that point it was a walk through dull modern suburbs, until I reached the narrow streets of the Old Town where the fiesta was obviously warming up, crammed with people, some in fancy dress, bands of musicians, and floats with effigies of St James and other figures. The noise was deafening and it was a relief to emerge into the relative calm of the vast square in front of the cathedral.

Built and repaired over many centuries, it is a combination of Romanesque and Gothic architecture, with a high altar that is a Baroque sculptural fantasy. St James the Moorslayer charges with sword drawn above the canopy, under which St James the Pilgrim, encased in silver and gold plate, presides over the sanctuary like a pagan idol. The custom for pilgrims, which I dutifully performed, is to climb the steps behind the altar and embrace the saint's waist from behind, giving thanks for a safe arrival.

The cathedral is also a working church serving many devout Catholics, and there is no better place than its pews to ponder the long and tangled history of the pilgrimage: a mixture of piety, superstition and nationalistic sentiment, enhanced by magnificent art and architecture – all inspired by the legend that St James, one of the original twelve disciples of Jesus, spread the Good News of Christianity in Spain for some years before returning to the Holy Land where he was martyred, and his remains were transported by boat (in some versions a stone boat) all the way to Galicia. This legend arose when Christians were contending with the Muslim Moors for dominance of the Iberian Peninsula, and finally succeeded in the fifteenth century. They needed a figurehead hero to compete with Mohammed, and a shrine to match the one in the Moorish city of Cordoba which boasted a relic of the prophet's arm. And that is how St James the Apostle became the patron saint of Spain.

I returned to the cathedral with the rest of the team a few days later on the 25th of July, the feast day of St James, for a High Mass celebrated by a phalanx of bishops in the presence of the Spanish royal family. On this occasion they were represented by Her Royal Highness Doña Pilar, sister of the king, who at the same hour was opening the Olympic Games in Barcelona, and probably having more fun. You had to claim your seat in the cathedral hours in advance, and by the time the service started most of the congregation were hot, tired and uncomfortable. What everybody was waiting for – Bill Megalos in particular – was the spectacle of the *Botofumeiro* – a giant golden censer trailing clouds of incense, suspended from the roof of the cathedral and swung high into the roof of the transept by six burly men in cassocks operating a complex tackle of ropes and pulleys. The one who had the task of stopping this holy Sputnik in its final swooping arc was lifted off his feet for a few moments and had to perform a little waltz on tiptoe to bring it to a halt. To me the spectacle had more than a touch of the circus about it.

The climax of the fiesta is an amazing display of fireworks in the cathedral square. Rockets erupt from the roof, from the three towers and every nook and cranny in the façade, drenching the whole structure in lurid light, so that it seems to be on fire. To me it was reminiscent of some of the apocalyptic paintings of Hieronymus Bosch, and also made me imagine what film footage of the Blitz in the City of London would have looked like in techni-colour. I was amazed that the authorities risked possible damage to the fabric of this unique building for the sake of the spectacle, but I presumed the pyrotechnicians were trusted masters of their craft.

When the fiesta is over many pilgrims go further, to Finisterre, the most westerly point of the European landmass, and in ancient times believed to be the end of the earth, as the name declares. We made our own way there one afternoon, sat near the edge of a high cliff overlooking the Atlantic Ocean, and watched the sun set over its shimmering, wave-wrinkled surface. The setting sun is an arche-typal image of death, of the separation of the soul from the body and its passage to the afterlife, a concept which predates Christian-ity. Beautiful, peaceful and elegiac, this scene provided the perfect conclusion to our film. Entitled *The Way of St James* in the BBC's Everyman series, it was transmitted early in 1993. A number of film documentaries about the Camino are currently listed on the inter-net, but ours is not included. It predated most, if not all of them, and was not released by the BBC as a commercial videotape or DVD, though copies can be retrieved online, I believe. As well as Bill Megalos' excellent camera work, it has a wonderfully evocative musical soundtrack. For years afterwards I received letters from people who had been prompted to walk or cycle parts of the Camino after seeing the TV programme, or reading *Therapy*, and had found the experience rewarding.

2

When I returned to England for the week's break from filming in Spain, I called Jack Temchin right away to catch up on developments with *The Writing Game*. His news was exciting. He had been in touch with Helen Mirren, who had recently made an impact in America for the first time with her performance in the British TV series *Prime Suspect*. Jack had heard that she was currently acting in a small repertory theatre in Los Angeles, but looking for a major role in a new play, and he had sent her the script of *The Writing Game*, which she agreed to read. I had admired her acting ever since I saw her feisty, sexy Cressida in *Troilus & Cressida* at Stratford-upon-Avon in 1968. She was now the right age to play Maude, and she had been at the top of my wish list for the part as soon as the prospect of a major production of the play appeared. Helen had called Jack to say she had read the play and thought it was very witty, but wasn't sure that Maude was 'a great part'. Jack had assured her that she would make it one, and Helen had invited him to go out to LA and discuss it over brunch at her home.

Early in August, when I was at home in Birmingham working on the script for the Santiago film, Jack called me to say jubilantly,

'We've got Helen Mirren!' He had just returned from LA where instead of brunch they had a three-hour restaurant dinner, and he said that the underlying assumption of their conversation was that she would do the play. She had read it for the third time and liked it 'more than ever', but now she feared the part of Leo was so good that it would take the play away from her. This struck me as a clever way of deferring commitment in the form of a compliment. Jack told her that male actors would have just the same reaction in reverse, which was why it was a good play. He seemed to have reassured her, because she referred him to her agent to discuss schedules. She was happy with Jack's suggestions for the casting of Leo in the New York production of *The Writing Game* – Ron Silver and Michael Douglas – and with Michael Bloom as director. She would soon be in England to film a sequel to *Prime Suspect*, and had given Jack her London phone number to pass on to me, which I thought was a good sign. I wrote in my diary: 'So there we are. A New York production with a star cast is now a real prospect. I should feel more elated than I am, but I have been through so many disappointments with this play in the past that I am wary of celebrating too soon.'

It was wise self-counselling. A few days later, when I knew Helen had arrived in England, I phoned her a couple of times and one evening she returned my call. Her theme was: 'Don't count on anything.' A long and difficult process lay ahead, and we would have to see if Jack Temchin could bring it to a successful conclusion. The main attraction of the play for her was the chance to act on the New York stage for the first time, and she was very anxious that it should be 'the right vehicle' for that purpose. I told Jack later that if he came up with a package of male star, theatre, and dates that she liked, I thought she would honour her verbal agreement, but if not, not.

I was not sanguine, but in mid-October, after a long silence from Jack which I thought ominous, there was some positive news relayed to me by my agent Leah Schmidt: Judd Hirsch, a well-known

21

actor, who was currently acting on Broadway in a hit play called *Conversations with my Father*, had read *The Writing Game*, and was sufficiently interested to suggest doing a private reading with Helen. Jack called me to confirm this and to say that she was very excited by the prospect of playing opposite him; also that her agent had read the play for the first time (rather belatedly, I thought) and loved it. During my brief stay in New York in April I had seen a play about a Jewish immigrant family in which Judd Hirsch had the leading role, and I thought he was brilliant. The omens looked good. Jack was worried that a private reading to a small invited audience might not go well, but Judd Hirsch made it a condition of his involvement, so the event was duly arranged for early December. Jack said that he couldn't pay to bring me over, but I said that wasn't a problem and I wouldn't want to miss it.

Early in November, Leah called to say that a producer called Peter Jeffries had made a proposal to film a staged production of *The Writing Game* for Channel 4, which Waldemar Januszczak, then head of its Arts Department (now better known as a leading art critic) had approved in principle. I said it would be fine by me, but that Jack Temchin would veto it as a violation of his rights in the piece, as indeed he did when consulted.

A couple of months earlier Chris Parr, who had produced the TV serial of *Nice Work*, had called me from America, where he was on location, with a new project: an adaptation of Charles Dickens' novel *Martin Chuzzlewit*. He had taken it with him to read on his trip, believed it had great potential for a TV serial, and wanted me to write the screenplay. I had to say that I had never read the book, which was a rather embarrassing confession. Dickens was one of my favourite writers, I had read all the other major novels, and I used to teach a 'Special Option' seminar course on Dickens in the Birmingham English Department, which I shared with my colleague, Ian Small. He taught *Martin Chuzzlewit* in our course, and

I had never found the time to read it myself. It had a mixed reception in its own day, and it is not a novel that found favour with either academic literary critics or the 'general reader' in modern times. However, I was attracted by the prospect of collaborating with Chris again on a major TV serial, and I said I would read the novel and let him know.

I thought coming to the book without any preconceptions could be an advantage for an adapter, and I was right. Although structurally flawed, perfectly fitting Henry James' disdainful characterisation of the typical nineteenth-century novel as a 'large, loose, baggy monster', I found it had marvellous things in it, and they were precisely the things that lend themselves readily to dramatic adaptation. Dickens' authorial voice – sardonic, prophetic and inventively metaphorical – is the dominant one in the great novels of his maturity such as *Bleak House* and *Little Dorrit*, but it cannot be included in an adaptation except by the intrusive use of voice-over. In *Martin Chuzzlewit* Dickens used his authorial voice sparingly, and made his characters reveal their natures by their actions, and above all by their words – the good characters by the transparent sincerity of their speech, and the morally deficient characters by their reliance on specious rhetoric. As always in Dickens, characters in the latter category, like Pecksniff and Mrs Gamp, are the most memorable. Throughout his life Dickens was addicted to the theatre, and tirelessly produced and acted in public and private performances of plays, some of which he wrote himself or in collaboration. Nowhere is the essentially theatrical nature of his genius as a novelist more evident than in *Martin Chuzzlewit*. There were many scenes in the novel, it seemed to me as I read it, that could be performed almost as written, and at least a dozen juicy roles of the kind that British actors excel in playing. As soon as I had finished reading the book, over 900 pages in the Penguin edition, I called Chris Parr to say yes. It was not an easy decision, for I was about to begin writing *Therapy* (as distinct from making notes about it) and taking on *Chuzzlewit* would entail at least six months of work. I told Chris that I wouldn't be available to begin on it until the spring of 1993, which he accepted.

I flew to New York on the 4th of December to attend the reading of *The Writing Game* with Helen Mirren and Judd Hirsch on the following evening. Jack called for me at my hotel at 5 p.m. and walked me to the venue, New Dramatists on 44th Street, a kind of club for aspiring playwrights with a small studio theatre where the event was to take place, so that I could get a feel for it. It was already dark and New York, which had seemed shabby and depressing when I arrived, was suddenly vibrant and exhilarating. It's something to do with the clear cold air in winter, very different from the damp, soupy atmosphere of London, which makes the canyons of skyscrapers, lit up from within against the night sky, a dazzling spectacle.

The reading was scheduled for 4 p.m. the next day and the cast gathered at 2.30. I met Helen Mirren for the first time and found her friendly and unaffected. She was looking extremely attractive, her blonde hair set off by a short red skirt, black tights and a white lace blouse with a plunging neckline, though it was not a costume Maude would have worn. About fifty people, almost a full house, turned up for the performance – a mixture of producers, investors and friends of the participants. Michael Bloom had got together a good cast for the minor roles, and the reading seemed to go well at first, with plenty of laughs. Helen was excellent, entirely plausible as a bestselling novelist, and showed she had a real gift for comedy. There's a passage where Leo declares, 'Most women, in my experience, don't believe their cunts are beautiful. That's why they keep their eyes shut when they write about sex,' and after a pause Maude says: 'I see.' (*another pause*) 'Well, now we know.' It was essential that this line should get a laugh to relieve the audience, especially women, of any discomfort they might feel at Leo's words, and I always waited for it in some suspense. Helen gave the definitive delivery of that second sentence, with the desired effect. But gradually it became obvious that Judd Hirsch had given very little preparation to the reading, and had little empathy with the play. He was all right in the early scenes, making clumsy attempts to seduce Maude, but he didn't seem to understand any of Leo's speeches about the craft and profession of writing, and his Leo never really seemed threatened by Simon St Clair's mockery, which deprived much of the second act of tension. Helen had spoken to me in the interval, about 'how well the play had read', but that couldn't be said of the second half.

The audience applauded generously at the end, and a number of people congratulated me, but I was disappointed. Helen went off quickly with Judd Hirsch to see his show that evening while Jack, Michael and I and a couple of backstage assistants found a café for an inquest over a drink and a snack. We agreed that Judd Hirsch was a good enough actor to make something of Leo, but he had behaved as if he wasn't really interested in playing the part, in which case we were no closer to getting the play on in New York. Jack summed up by saying that the reading hadn't done the play any harm, but I felt that it hadn't done the play any good either.

I returned to England assuming that Judd Hirsch would drop out, and so he did, as Jack confirmed at the end of December. But in the same telephone call he reported that the director of Long Wharf, a repertory theatre in New Haven, Connecticut, had offered to stage his production of *The Writing Game* if he could 'deliver' Helen Mirren. He seemed quite excited by this possibility, though I was not enthused by the prospect of another provincial venue. Leah however was in favour of pursuing it. She told me that Long Wharf was the most prestigious of American regional theatres and had the best record of moving shows to New York, and pointed out that Helen might be more inclined to take her chances with the play if it opened there first. In February of the New Year she reported that

Long Wharf had promised to put it on in January 1994 with the same condition of Helen Mirren's commitment, but with a further condition that Michael Bloom did not direct. No reason was given for this exclusion but there was some suspicion that the artistic director of the theatre fancied the job himself. I was reluctant to agree out of loyalty to Michael, but Leah persuaded me not to be so scrupulous because this sort of thing happened all the time in the theatre world. I asked Jack if Mike Ockrent might be invited to direct, thinking Michael Bloom would recognise his superior status and not be offended. Jack was certain that Long Wharf would not be interested but said that the Manhattan Theatre Club, and other prestigious off-Broadway theatres, would jump at it if Helen were also involved and urged me to sound out Mike Ockrent. It was no surprise to me that he declined because of other commitments, but he was delighted that *The Writing Game* was still attracting interest. I promised to tell him the whole saga one day, and he said, 'You must write a book about it.'

Mary and I took a week's holiday in Crete at Easter, our first visit. We hired a car and drove around, struck by the number of new houses under construction which were open to the sky after the first floor. Whether this was evidence of a boom or a collapse in property one could not tell, but I thought it was probably the latter. We found a friendly but rather chaotic hotel which was just opening up for the tourist season and overlooked an attractive beach and bay, but the weather and the water were not warm enough to encourage swimming. We went to Iraklion and in the museum there I found some absorbing displays and information about the events of the Second World War on the island, in which British servicemen (including Evelyn Waugh) were involved. But the most memorable sight-seeing experience was inevitably the prehistoric Palace of Knossos, which we reserved for our last day. Superbly restored and presented, it alone made the trip worthwhile.

When we got home on the 14th of April I found a letter from Leah dated the 8th in my mail, beginning: 'Good news! Helen Mirren has committed to the Long Wharf and is prepared to allow them to announce her as star of the play.' After savouring this message with intense pleasure for a couple of hours I called Jack, who sadly informed me that on the very same day that the announcement appeared in the press, the Long Wharf got a call from Helen's agent to say that she was backing out. She was replacing Judi Dench in the current London production of Peter Shaffer's new play, *The Gift of the Gorgon*, and going with it to Broadway. The only good thing about this debacle was that it happened before Jack reached the point of telling Michael Bloom he wasn't going to direct my play at the Long Wharf, which might have caused a permanent breach between him and us.

And so it went on, throughout 1993 and into 1994 and 1995, this epic effort to stage a top-class production of *The Writing Game* in America. We did not attempt to woo Helen Mirren any more, but a long series of other actresses were proposed by various interested people and approached through their agents: Judy Davis, Lynn Redgrave, Kate Nelligan, Zoë Wanamaker, Meryl Streep, Mia Farrow, Juliet Stevenson, Eileen Atkins, Maria Aitken ... and more. For some time there was a project for a new British production with a husband and wife team, Michael Brandon and Glynis Barber (he American, she English) who had starred in the popular TV detective series *Dempsey & Makepeace*, playing Leo and Maude. The play was to open with a provincial tour and hopefully finish in the West End, but it never materialised for reasons I don't remember. Offers were also made to well-known male actors to play the part of Leo which seemed promising but came to nothing. So much activity, so many meetings, phone calls, letters and faxes (email had not yet established itself as a universal medium of communication) with such little result. I wondered how the people involved managed to make a living out of this perpetually frustrating activity, but somehow they did. Jack Temchin renewed his option for another year in May 1994, $3000 in two instalments.

In April 1994 I booked to see Helen Mirren in Turgenev's *A Month in the Country* at the Albery Theatre in the West End, and sent a note to her there giving the date and asking if we might meet after the show. I wrote: 'I won't disguise the fact that I would like to sound you out on the subject of *The Writing Game*, but I promise not to be boringly insistent.' I was disappointed that she did not reply. I thought she owed it to me. But I went to the play anyway, and she was predictably brilliant as Natalya Petrovna.

It was the end of my connection with Helen Mirren, but not of my involvement in the fortunes of *The Writing Game*. In the spring of 1995 Waldemar Januszczak's proposal to film a staged version for Channel 4 mutated into the more appealing concept of a ninety-minute TV play recorded in a studio with some additional exterior film sequences, and I was commissioned to write the script. As Jack Temchin's option had finally expired, I was free to do so. This was a very satisfying project to work on, and it developed at an unusually fast pace. It was greenlighted after a meeting between Waldemar, the producer Michael Custance, the veteran director Stuart Burge, and me. Michael drew up a schedule based on the availability of Stuart which meant beginning rehearsals on the 24th of May and recording over four days in June immediately before I was due to travel to Nice with Mary to take part in a Nabokov conference organized by Maurice Couturier, with a week's holiday added on. I delivered the first draft of the script for discussion in April. It began like the play with Leo escorted into the barn by Jeremy, but Stuart suggested it should begin with the character of Penny who, he rightly said, was the character with whom the audience was most likely to identify. I rewrote the opening scene for the second draft as soon as I got home: Penny, having arrived early for the creative writing course, cautiously enters the empty barn and is accosted by the manager Jeremy coming down the stairs. He explains that this building is the tutors' accommodation, and she says, 'How do they do it?'

JEREMY: Do it?

PENNY: Teach you to write.

JEREMY: Ah well, that depends. Did you bring anything with you?

PENNY: Yes, the opening chapter of my novel.

JEREMY: Well, they'll probably begin by discussing that, and then go on from there . . .

I integrated this opening into the text for every subsequent production of the play, and discovered other opportunities for improving it through working on the TV adaptation.

The next thing to be addressed was casting. Stuart Burge had a great admiration for the actress Susan Wooldridge and wanted to have the experience of working with her before his imminent retirement. I had never seen her on the stage or in *The Jewel in the Crown*, a popular ITV series about the last years of British rule in India, but I knew she had won several prestigious acting awards and agreed that she should be top of the list for Maude. We were also unanimous that we needed an American actor for Leo, and in spite of the discouraging experience of casting this part for the Birmingham Rep we aimed high. The first approach was made to Elliott Gould, well known for his appearance in films like *Ted and Carol and Bob and Alice* and *M*A*S*H*. I was impressed that Michael Custance was able to speak to him in Los Angeles within a few hours of contacting his agent. He was definitely interested, and the script was couriered to him immediately. He faxed Michael to say he was rarely offered parts as rich as Leo and he would have loved to do it if he hadn't been committed to a film schedule that clashed with ours. When Michael phoned him to express regret

29

and ask if he had any alternative names to suggest, he anticipated the question instantly: 'I know what you're going to say. I'm going to meet George Segal in the next forty-eight hours and I'll talk to him about it.' He called back to say that Segal was interested and he had biked the script over to him. Michael Custance was almost in tears of gratitude for this unselfish co-operation. Within a few days George Segal accepted and said he couldn't wait to play the part.

I had discovered that the budget for this production was only £165,000, a small sum, it seemed to me, for a ninety-minute TV play with additional filming on location, and I feared that George Segal would require too large a slice of it. But in fact he didn't want a fee – just to be well looked after and accommodated in a first-class hotel. He was doing the whole thing for the pleasure of exercising his craft, and throughout the making of the film he was delightful company. The contrast with our efforts to cast Helen Mirren in *The Writing Game* in America could not have been starker or more gratifying. Of course, as I learned from experience, casting stage plays is always a more complex process than casting for television drama. The former have to be planned long ahead of opening, and may have long runs, tying down the actors in ways which might prevent them from taking more attractive offers later. Our production would be ready to go in a matter of weeks, and finished in a few more, so if an actor was available and the part attractive, he or she would commit readily.

When we began to interview actors for the other parts I was surprised by the high calibre of those who responded to invitations. A respected film actress was keen to play Maude, but her studio would not release her, so Stuart's choice of Susan Wooldridge for Maude was endorsed. Michael Maloney was cast as Simon St Clair, which delighted me. I knew his work and could imagine him doing the part wonderfully, as he did at the very first read-through. I also met the actor playing Jeremy for the first time on that occasion, and was pleasantly surprised to find he was

Ralph Nossek, who had been in the cast of the revue *Slap in the Middle* at the Birmingham Rep in 1962, my very first involvement in professional live theatre. I felt the coincidence was propitious. The part of Penny, the primary school teacher, was the last to be filled, by a little-known young actress from Northern Ireland called Zara Turner, who seemed to possess in herself the perfect combination of qualities for the role: acumen, sincerity, and beauty. Later she would have a successful career as a lead actress in television and film. Considering the constraints of our budget, it was a very strong cast.

The play was recorded in a TV studio in Southampton which was cheaply available because its multicamera equipment had been overtaken by more advanced technology, but it was exactly what we needed. The technicians with the knowhow to operate it had to be tracked down in their enforced retirement, but they seemed pleased to return to their old workplace and were very co-operative. Michael found an attractive rustic farm in the area whose owner was willing to let us film external shots of the characters arriving and walking in and out of the buildings before we started recording in the studio. For budgetary reasons we had a tight schedule. The studio was hired for four days, and recording had to finish on the fourth day with no possibility of extension. To my intense regret I was unable to witness the last day's work, because I had to fly to Nice to join the Nabokov conference, and I only learned what an epic achievement the completion of the recording was when I returned from France two weeks later.

I called Michael as soon as I was home, and he told me the story of the last day. They began recording at 9 a.m. and went on continuously until it was obvious to him that they would not get to the end of the script until 2 a.m. the next day. He told the crew and technicians that they were going to overrun unless they shot the rest of the piece in wide angle, without any finesse; or alternatively they could do it properly in as much time as it took, and they all voted to do the job properly. Needless to say there was no money for overtime pay available, but Michael ordered beer and pizzas to keep the team going. George and Sue did their final scene together in an uninterrupted eleven-minute take, and everyone collapsed in tired relief except, amazingly, Stuart Burge who at seventy-seven was the oldest person involved. When I saw the first edited version of the play George looked slightly drowsy at times in his last scene with Susan, but it so happened that in the script he has only just got out of bed at that point and is wearing a dressing gown, so his sleepy expression seemed appropriate.

When I saw a fully edited tape of the play, and again when I watched it transmitted on Channel 4, many things in it delighted me, but it confirmed an uneasy feeling I had had all along, that Susan Wooldridge was not ideal casting for Maude. She certainly looked beautiful enough to excite Leo's interest on first sight, and her exquisite English upper-middle-class manners and speech contrasted amusingly with Leo's coarser character and vocabulary, but it was hard to believe that this Maude would tacitly invite Leo to take a shower with her after two days' acquaintance. They worked together very well as a pair on the level of light comedy, but I missed something – or perhaps someone: Helen Mirren, and what she might have done with the role in this medium.

For programming reasons the TV transmission of the play was delayed until Sunday the 18th of February, 1996. Preview comments in the press were encouraging, and against strong competition on other channels that evening *The Writing Game* attracted an estimated 1.2 million viewers, which was considered a good result (and roughly equivalent to a full house at the Birmingham Rep six nights a week for four and a half years). The reviews were mostly favourable though few in number. To my disappointment, the programme was never repeated by Channel 4. I watched the VHS tape recording for the first time in a very long while when writing these pages, and it struck me that the compression of the original play into ninety minutes made an uncustomary demand on the viewer's concentration. There are many long speeches in it, and because all the characters are writers, many long words in them. TV drama as a medium prefers short lines and expressive visuals. This difference between drama on stage and on television has become still more marked since 1996, as the latter has become formally indistinguishable from feature films.

3

If the preceding chapter gave the impression that my professional life was dominated by *The Writing Game* in the years 1992–5, it was misleading. I was only intermittently involved in the ongoing saga of the play's fortunes and misfortunes in that period, and mainly preoccupied with two new projects: my novel *Therapy* and the TV adaptation of *Martin Chuzzlewit*. I had decided to make the novel's central character, Tubby Passmore, the writer of a long-running television situation comedy, and although I had experience of writing screenplays for television, and had been involved in the production of *Nice Work*, I knew little about sitcoms apart from watching some occasionally, so I had to do research into the way they were made. Someone suggested I should contact Martin Shardlow, a veteran director of sitcoms such as *Coming Home* and *Blackadder*, who was currently in charge of one called *The Upper Hand*, produced for ITV by Central Television at their East Midlands studios in Nottingham. I explained that I wanted to write a novel about a sitcom scriptwriter and asked Martin if I could observe his show in production. He kindly agreed, and allowed me to watch rehearsals and recordings of *The Upper Hand*, a process which was completely different from the making of *Nice Work*. The typical sitcom is acted on a stage set in front of an audience whose laughter (primed by a 'warm-up' comedian before the recording starts) hopefully stimulates the amusement of the viewers in their homes. The action of a single episode, normally thirty minutes long, is recorded simultaneously by several cameramen in different positions, whose shots are selected and combined by the director or his assistants, sitting in the control room in front of a range of small screens. *The Upper Hand* was a British adaptation of an American original and had a simple structure: a widower with several young children applies for the job of resident housekeeper to an affluent single businesswoman and is taken on, mainly due to the influence of her mother. Small domestic crises of a comic nature involving both families provide the dramatic momentum, but what engages the audience is that the employer and employee, who quarrel constantly, obviously fancy each other without admitting it. As Martin remarked, the series was kept going by a constant '*will-they–won't-they?*' question underlying the action. It was a simple but effective formula, and the series had a very long run.

The sitcom I invented for Tubby Passmore is called *The People Next Door* and owes something in structure to my observation of *The Upper Hand*. An affluent couple with children who occupy an expensive terrace townhouse in London are dismayed when a working-class family inherits the house on the other side of the party wall, and moves in. There is friction between the two pairs of parents, with their very different values and life-styles, though the children fraternise. Early in the novel Tubby is alarmed by the threatened defection of the actress playing the posh wife, who is the star of the show but wants to return to working in live theatre as soon as the series reaches the end of its run. This jeopardises the chances of another series being commissioned, and ratchets up his anxiety to new heights. As well as trying various therapies, Tubby relieves his stress by writing an occasional journal about his experiences and worries, and most of the novel is narrated in this form, in a colloquial style which retains the tone of his working-class upbringing in south-east London, where his father was a tram driver, and is peppered with the kind of jokes and wordplay appropriate to his profession. But as I got further into the composition of the book I began to fear that the blokish vernacular style of Tubby's journal could become tiresome, and felt I needed the presence of another kind of discourse which would contrast with Tubby's, more literary and more sophisticated but also relevant to his psychological problems. That was how Kierkegaard came into the book.

A few years earlier when I was preparing to write *Paradise News*, with a Catholic priest who lost his faith and left the Church as its central character, I read a number of books about theology and religion. One of them was Walter Lowrie's *A Short Life of Kierkegaard*, my first and so far only source of information about the Danish philosopher. Some fragmentary memories of that book made me think that it might provide the second level of discourse I needed, and when I read it again my hunch was confirmed. All his life Kierkegaard was a prey to depression, though he usually called it 'melancholy', and to acute anxiety, for which he borrowed the German word *Angst*. Early in the novel Tubby's friend Amy comes to his London flat for a drink and asks him, 'How's the knee? And how's the angst?' Tubby is not at all sure what 'angst' is, and looks it up later in his English dictionary which tells him it is '*An acute but unspecific sense of anxiety or remorse*' especially associated with the philosophy of Existentialism, which leads him to its originator, Søren Kierkegaard. Tubby looks up Kierkegaard in a biographical dictionary and makes notes in his journal:

He was the son of a self-made merchant and inherited a considerable fortune from his father. He spent it all on studying philosophy and religion. He was engaged to a girl called Regine but broke it off because he decided he wasn't suited to marriage. Apart from a couple of spells in Berlin, he never left Copenhagen. His life sounded as dull as it was short. But the article listed some of his books at the end. I can't describe how I felt as I read the titles. If the hairs on the back of my neck were shorter, they would have lifted. *Fear and Trembling*, *The Sickness unto Death*, *The Concept of Dread* – they didn't sound like the titles of philosophy books, they seemed to name my condition like arrows thudding into a target. Even the ones I couldn't understand or guess at the contents of, like *Either/Or* and *Repetition*, seemed pregnant with hidden meaning designed especially for me. And what do you know – Kierkegaard wrote a Journal! I must get hold of it, and some of the other books.

Tubby is intelligent but not intellectual. He scraped through the eleven plus as a boy. His secondary education was in a stuffy grammar school which he disliked and left at the age of sixteen with undistinguished O levels. His only success at school was as a comic actor in the annual play. He took an office job with a theatrical agency, which led him to apply to drama school. He worked for some years as an actor in provincial rep, but found more success as a writer of comic sketches, and finally sitcoms, for television. I thought there were possibilities for humour, and also for pathos, in the portrayal of such a man struggling with the paradoxes and complexities of Kierkegaard's thought in an effort to understand why he isn't happy.

At an early stage of work on this novel I took Mary with me for a short break in Copenhagen, which neither of us had been to before, to get some sense of the environment in which Kierkegaard lived for most of his life, and in particular to visit the City Museum where there was a room dedicated to various pieces of furniture, documents and other memorabilia that belonged or referred to him. I still have pinned to the corkboard in my study the postcard reproduction of a portrait of Regine Olsen, his first and only love, which I brought back from that trip. When I re-read Walter Lowrie's biography of Kierkegaard I was particularly interested in the story of his characteristically self-torturing relationship with Regine. She loved him as much as he loved her, but he wouldn't marry her because he believed he couldn't make her happy. She was unable to persuade him otherwise, and eventually she despaired and broke off their engagement. In due course another man courted her and she married him. Kierkegaard spent the rest of his life regretting his decision, but never stopped loving Regine.

This poignant story gave me the idea that Tubby might have had a first love in adolescence whom he rejected for some reason, and belatedly realises in middle age that he acted badly. His marriage to Sally is under strain because of his moodiness and abstraction, and he is seized with a desire to track down his former sweetheart and express regret and contrition for the way they parted. This quest takes him back to the south-east London suburb where he grew up and met a Catholic schoolgirl called Maureen who became his sweetheart until he broke off the relationship, but his efforts to find her again in middle age lead him further afield and eventually to the Camino de Compostela.

I would not have thought of sending my character to Spain and Santiago if I had not been there recently myself. I'm sure many novelists draw on experiences of their own that are still fresh in the memory and splice them into the fictional narratives on which they are working. When to my dismay the pain in my knee joint returned some months after my operation, which was supposed to have been a success, I went to see my physiotherapist to ask him what the problem could be. 'It's probably Internal Derangement of the Knee,' he said with a sardonic smile. 'That's what the orthopaedic surgeons call it between themselves. I.D.K. for short. I Don't Know.' That went straight into the novel, and 'I.D.K.' became a recurrent motif in Tubby's thoughtstream, applicable to all kinds of bafflement and frustration.

When I was staying in my flat near Leicester Square I was very conscious of the number of people, often young people, who were sleeping rough in the West End, wrapped in sleeping bags in the porches and under the canopies of shops and theatres. Like many other Londoners, no doubt, I felt both pity for these people and a certain irritation at having to step around or over them on occasion. The building in which my flat was situated had a small entry porch, and for a time a young man made the pavement to one side of it his nocturnal base. He was very polite and always moved out of the way if I had occasion to go in or out at night, but I resented his presence and probably showed it. Occasionally police patrols moved these street people on, and sometimes there would be friction between them. This prompted me to weave a new plot strand into the novel.

Tubby leaves his building one evening to find a young man whom he has observed from his flat on the entryphone's video-screen squatting in the porch and tells him to get out. In the argument that follows the young man displays an unexpected range of slightly muddled high-cultural references which surprise and intrigue Tubby. When two policemen come up and ask, 'Anything wrong sir?' Tubby impulsively pretends that he knows the young man, and to demonstrate it takes him into his flat, instantly deconstructing his decision in Kierkegaardian mode (*'If you shop him you will regret it, if you don't shop him you will regret it, shop him or don't shop him, you will regret both.'*) The thread of this unlikely relationship runs through the rest of the novel till the very end. In retrospect, for I wasn't conscious of it at the time, I think this episode, and the plot strand that develops from it, owes something to my saturation in Dickens' novels through teaching the course at Birmingham University and working on the TV adaptation of *Martin Chuzzlewit*. The novels are full of compassion for the plight of the poor and destitute in Victorian London, whose gaslit pavements and sordid slums Dickens often patrolled at night. He had a particular concern for the plight of prostitutes, rescuing many of them from the streets and founding a refuge for them out of his own pocket. Tubby's protective reaction to the squatter in his porch echoes similar situations in Dickens, and the youth himself is something of a Dickensian character, with traits in common with the Artful Dodger.

I kept my promise to Chris Parr that I would make a start on the adaptation of *Martin Chuzzlewit* in the spring of 1993. I had intended to work on both the screenplay and the novel in tandem, but as soon as I started on *Chuzzlewit* it became an all-consuming project, and I resigned myself to putting *Therapy* aside for a while. I had been fooling myself in pretending I could do otherwise. Creative writing doesn't just go on at your desk. It goes on inside your head intermittently throughout your waking hours, as you turn over the problems and possibilities of the work in progress, and some of your best ideas may come in that way. You can't maintain this ruminative, receptive state of mind in respect of two quite different large-scale projects. At least, I can't.

Dickens' novel is a long rambling narrative set in England at an unspecified time before the Railway Age began in the late 1830s (all journeys are made with horses or on foot) and has a great many characters and interwoven plot lines. There are two Martin Chuzzlewits: the older is a wealthy and misanthropic gentleman who has brought up an orphan, Mary Graham, to look after him, and the younger is his grandson, who falls in love with Mary and wants to marry her. This causes old Martin to disown him, so young Martin apprentices himself to the architect Mr Pecksniff, a cousin of the Chuzzlewits and a career hypocrite, who lives in a country village with his two daughters, Mercy and Charity. There is also an Anthony Chuzzlewit, ailing brother to old Martin, who has a villainous son called Jonas. He poisons his father in order to inherit his fortune, marries Mercy and makes her life miserable, collaborates in an insurance swindle and finally kills himself. In the meantime young Martin is dismissed by Pecksniff and goes to America to make his fortune, but nearly dies of fever there, while Pecksniff takes advantage of his absence to make unwelcome advances to Mary, who has long been the secret object of undeclared love by Tom Pinch, Pecksniff's selfless and much exploited retainer.

In the course of the story Pecksniff takes his daughters to London to further plots of his own, staying at a lodging house for single gentlemen called Todgers's after the proprietor Mrs Todgers. To a modern reader this name in its context inevitably suggests a ribald play on words, but I was unable to convince Pedr James, the director, that 'todger' was not a slang term for penis before the twentieth century. Dickens in fact scrupulously abstained from sexual innuendo in all his work, but he did have some fun with the impact of the two young Pecksniff girls' temporary residence at Todgers's on its male occupants, one of whom was very well acted in our serial by a young man called Julian Fellowes, now known as Lord Fellowes, the creator and writer of the popular TV series *Downton Abbey*. This part of Dickens' book contains some of its most amusing scenes, but I had to abbreviate them because there was simply not enough screen time to include them in full.

Several new characters are introduced in London, including Mrs Gamp. 'She was a fat old woman, Mrs Gamp, with a husky voice and a moist eye ... Having very little neck, it cost her some trouble to look over herself, if one may say so, at those to whom she talked.' Mrs Gamp would be looking over her large bosom at them, being employed to sit with invalids, and 'lay out' corpses awaiting burial, sustained by tipples of strong liquor. She justifies herself by frequently quoting conversations with a patron of hers, a Mrs Harris, who is never seen and probably never existed. E.g., 'Mrs Harris,' I says, 'leave the bottle on the chimley piece, and don't ask me to take none, but let me put my lips to it when I am so dispoged, and then I will do what I'm engaged to do.' Nowhere is Dickens' comic genius more brilliantly displayed than in his characterisation of Mrs Gamp. She was so popular with readers of the first edition of the novel, which was published in monthly instalments, that he made her a much more prominent figure than he had originally intended. All Dickens' novels were first published in monthly pamphlets, or as long-running serials in magazines, and he was often influenced in developing his stories by the ongoing audience reaction. He sent young Martin to America with his faithful servant and friend Mark Tapley because sales of the monthly instalments were falling and he had a lot of material in the notes he had kept during a visit to America in 1842 which he thought would enliven the story. He had been lionised there at first, but soon became disillusioned and disgusted by many aspects of American society, which he expressed in set-pieces satirising American stereotypes in his novel, causing much resentment in the New World and not greatly improving his sales in the Old.

When I began the work of adapting *Martin Chuzzlewit*, Chris Parr encouraged me to do it freely rather than faithfully, and indeed there was no alternative. Adapting a novel for film or television is always a process of judicious condensation and deletion, if only because it usually takes longer in real time to deliver a speech or perform an action than it does to read a verbal description of the same, but *Martin Chuzzlewit* required more drastic cutting than most. It was so loosely constructed that Dickens himself seemed to have lost the plot at times. I was asked to list the seasons of the year at which particular scenes and sequences in the story were taking place, to ensure that the weather, settings, costumes, etc. would seem appropriate when filmed. This proved quite difficult because I discovered two different and incompatible calendars in the story. For instance, young Martin's apprenticeship to Pecksniff appears from close scrutiny of the text to last no more than a few days before he sets off to make his fortune in

America as an architect, and he seems to return to England in winter in one chapter, but at high summer in another. Not that this matters in the least: *Martin Chuzzlewit* is not a realistic novel and few readers notice such anomalies in its extraordinarily long and complex narrative. It reminded me often of Shakespeare's plays, especially the late ones, like *The Winter's Tale*, *Cymbeline*, and *The Tempest*, whose plots are derived from the romance tradition and written to display extremes of good and evil and the ultimate triumph of the former over the latter. I was delighted when I discovered later that Dickens took a compact edition of Shakespeare's plays with him when he went to America, a parting gift from his friend John Foster, and carried it everywhere with him on his travels; and that *Chuzzlewit* contains more Shakespearian quotations and allusions than any other of his novels.

The most obvious target for drastic cuts in the narrative was the long American section, and some in the production team thought it should be omitted altogether, but I demurred. Young Martin's near death from fever in the swampy land in the far West which he had been tricked into buying, from which he is nursed back to health by Mark, is the turning point in young Martin's life, the beginning of his renunciation of selfishness, the vice which Dickens said was the underlying theme of the whole novel. We could not cut the entire episode, but I found a way to represent it economically using letters sent by Martin and read by Mary, intercut with scenes from the swamp which were filmed in a flooded quarry in Gloucestershire.

By August, after a good many drafts, I had written a complete script which satisfied Chris Parr and the rest of the team. Meanwhile Chris had been made Head of TV Drama at Pebble Mill, which gave him additional influence with the BBC hierarchy in London. The screenplay was soon greenlighted for production in a format of five episodes of fifty minutes. The next stage in this process is the appointment of a director, who is responsible for the realisation of the script in performance. Ideally the director and writer should collaborate from the beginning of such a project, but this rarely happens. The writer must therefore expect to do more work on it once the director is involved. Chris Parr, after consultation with Mike Wearing, who was now Head of Series and Serials in London, had appointed Pedr James, an experienced director who had been working in television since the 1970s. He was well known for TV dramas on contemporary subjects, especially an enchanting film about a schoolkids' outing to the seaside, *Our Day Out*. He had never directed the adaptation of a classic novel before, and it was hoped that he would broaden the audience for this genre. He and I had a wary conversation on the phone in which he said some vaguely complimentary things about the script, but more emphatically: 'Chris tells me that you're very professional about doing rewrites.' He took Dickens' novel and the script with him to his country cottage in Wales and came back two weeks later with twenty closely typed A4 pages of notes on the first two episodes alone.

His principal criticism of my screenplay was that it did not follow Dickens' narrative faithfully and undervalued the 'good' characters, especially Tom Pinch, the much-exploited assistant of Pecksniff and the humble, undeclared lover of Mary. I acknowledged that I may have not given Tom Pinch his due, and willingly expanded his role, which was beautifully performed by Philip Franks, who nobly submitted to having his head shaved to correspond to Dickens' description of Pinch as 'prematurely bald' and Hablot Browne's illustration for the first edition of the novel. But there was no way I could incorporate all Pedr's desired rewrites in a 5 x 50-minute serial. This problem was partly solved when Chris and Pedr persuaded Michael Jackson, the controller of BBC2, to let us have some additional screen time – with the catch that it had to be accomplished within the original agreed budget. This we managed mainly by cutting down on scenic outdoor sequences, which in fact the story, packed with drama and great characters, didn't need. We were able to extend the first episode from the usual sixty minutes to ninety, getting the audience thoroughly familiar with the main characters and their relationships, and ending on a suspenseful turning point in the story.

A wonderful cast was assembled by drawing on the experience of Pedr James and Chris Parr and inviting other members of the team to make suggestions. The role of old Martin Chuzzlewit was offered to Paul Scofield who accepted, much to my own joy at having one of the finest Shakespearian actors of the age in our adaptation of Dickens' most Shakespearian novel. He was also a very congenial man to work with, totally committed to the task. There is a moment in the story when the villainous Jonas (played with relish by Keith Allen), the unsuspected murderer of his father Anthony Chuzzlewit, is startled by the sudden appearance of his uncle, old Martin. Dickens describes 'a ghastly change in Jonas' at this moment, which I thought was hinting at a family resemblance that made Jonas think he was seeing his father's ghost, and I gave him a line to this effect. Pedr liked this idea, and realising that the two Chuzzlewit brothers never appeared in the same scene in the screenplay, invited Paul Scofield to play both of them, which he did so effectively that few viewers of the serial would have guessed until the credits rolled. There is an old man in Jonas' ménage, known as Mr Chuffey, once a clerk in the family business, now an almost senile retainer routinely abused by Jonas, who makes occasional cryptic remarks about the family's history. The film star John Mills, who was himself eighty-five at the time, was shrewdly selected to play the part of Chuffey and created a memorable and deeply moving character.

Tom Wilkinson was cast as Pecksniff. I had always thought that the success of our show would depend crucially on the portrayal of this character, who has far more lines than any other in the screenplay, and it was a great relief to see how, from the very first read-through onwards, Tom seized the part as if he had been waiting all his professional life for the opportunity, and made it his own. His Pecksniff was wonderfully loathsome and yet irresistibly magnetising, as he had to be if his success in deceiving others with his unctuous rhetoric was to be credible. Pecksniff's daughters Charity and Mercy were brilliantly portrayed by Emma Chambers and Julia Sawalha, who had already made names for themselves in two popular TV series, *The Vicar of Dibley* and *Absolutely Fabulous*.

The casting of Mrs Gamp was more contentious. Like most members of the team, I was in favour of Miriam Margolyes, whose monologues in the persona of Mrs Gamp were famous, but Pedr was against this for reasons he never spelled out, and instead he cast Elizabeth Spriggs, a distinguished actress who had performed often with the Royal Shakespeare Company. Miriam Margolyes, who obviously felt she had something of a proprietary right to the part, was furious when she heard about this casting, and apparently phoned Pedr more than once, trying to persuade him in the husky voice and illiterate Cockney idiolect of Dickens' character to change his mind – but in vain. Elizabeth Spriggs adroitly disguised her own natural stateliness, and imitated the speech and mannerisms of Mrs Gamp very accurately; but I couldn't help regretting Margolyes' absence. Pete Postlethwaite joined the cast late in the shooting schedule to deliver a barnstorming performance as Montague Tigg, the head of a crooked insurance business, who lures both Jonas and Pecksniff into investing a large amount of money which they soon lose when the firm collapses. I thought this would ring some bells with a modern audience, and invented a conversation between the men in which Pecksniff asks anxiously, 'But is it safe?' and Tigg answers, 'As safe as Lloyds.'[1]

---

[1] Investors in this venerable institution suffered serious losses in 1991 as a result of massive claims from the USA connected with the use of asbestos in the building industry.

*

Because of the limited time available for rehearsals, and the length of the screenplay, Pedr did not attempt to rehearse the acting of scenes. Instead, after the first collective read-through, the cast of each scene sat around a long table and read the script, discussed it, analysed it, and read it again. It was like a seminar in which every participant was totally focussed – something I never experienced as a teacher, and very educative for me. Tom Wilkinson, who had acquired a kind of natural authority in these sessions, brought one of them to a close by commenting that usually these read-throughs were extended by quibbles and arguments about the meaning or effectiveness of particular lines and speeches, but that day they had sailed through it with ease and finished earlier than usual, which he throught was a sign that it was a good script. There was a murmur of agreement, which was of course very gratifying to me.

There was only one actor in the cast about whom I had any reservations, and that was Ben Walden, chosen by Pedr to play the part of young Martin. At the first read-through he looked intimidated by the talent around the table, and delivered his lines in a low voice, stumbling over them occasionally. He did not noticeably improve. He was short and slight in stature and not especially handsome. There were a score of young actors who could have played the part, and Pedr must have auditioned several of them, but he chose Ben, and I couldn't help wondering why, until somebody told me the background story. He was the son of Brian Walden, a Member of Parliament well known for his outspoken journalism and books, who apparently disapproved of Ben's choice of career, and there was a serious breach between them when Ben decided to go to America and join the famous Method School of Acting in New York founded by Lee Strasberg. When Pedr heard this story from Ben he was fascinated by its parallels with old Martin Chuzzlewit's relationship with his grandson, and thought that Ben could draw on his own experience to give emotional depth to the character of young Martin. I believed this to be a serious misjudgement, and so did everybody else in the cast I spoke to. I tried privately to persuade Pedr to replace Ben as soon as possible, before it became public knowledge that he had been in the cast, but Pedr was adamant. In the event Ben was just about adequate in his role, but he was the only actor in the huge cast who attracted any negative comment in reviews. Happily he was reconciled with his father, and had a career as an actor for several years before moving into the field of education.

4

The filming of *Martin Chuzzlewit* began in mid-February 1994, when I was due to travel to Australia to take part in the Writers' Week of the annual Adelaide Festival, but I managed to observe the first two days' work in and around a picturesque old pub in the countryside near Birmingham which stood in for the Blue Dragon Inn of Dickens' novel. It was a bright cold day, with a thin layer of snow on the ground and on the roofs of the inn and the nearby village church. The action at this point was supposed to be taking place in midwinter, and I thought it auspicious that Nature was kindly co-operating with us. But I was looking forward to some warm sunshine in Australia.

I had received the invitation to Adelaide nine months earlier, and accepted it because I had heard good reports from other authors of the Writers' Week and also because both of my fiction publishers, Secker & Warburg and Penguin, were expanding their operations in Australia and were keen that I should go there. They shared the cost of my travel and agreed to pay for business class for the long flight to and from Sydney. From there it was a relatively short flight to Melbourne, where a couple of engagements at the University had been arranged, and then on to Adelaide. The Festival humanely offers new arrivals travelling such long distances several days rest at a ranch in the country outside the city before they are required to perform. The English contingent included Penelope Lively and Nicholas Shakespeare. I was particularly pleased to make the acquaintance of Penelope for the first time, and enjoyed her company on several strolls and excursions. Nicholas was the son of the British Ambassador to Peru, and had spent some time in that country. He wrote a powerful novel called *The Vision of Elena Silves* about the vicious armed conflict there between the state and Marxist guerrillas. It was submitted for the Booker Prize in 1989, and as chair of the judges I thought it was a contender, but it didn't make the shortlist. One day we were taken on a guided walk through a nature reserve with delightful koala bears in the trees and wallabies hopping about underneath them. At some point we were joined by an attractive young woman, slim and dark-haired, who smiled a lot but said very little. Nobody introduced her and it was only later that we discovered she was Donna Tartt, the American author of a fabulously successful novel, *The Secret History*, published in 1992, and that she and Nicholas were an item. She took no official part in the Festival programme.

Having brought us all this way, the organisers of the Writers' Week understandably kept us busy after we left the ranch and transferred to hotels in the city. We appeared, singly and in groups, in marquees and sometimes in the open air, to discuss the state of the British novel and to be interviewed individually about our own work. Penguin had timed the publication of their one-volume edition of my 'Rummidge Trilogy' (*Changing Places*, *Small World* and *Nice Work*) to coincide with the Festival, but I had no new novel to promote. I was reluctant to reveal much about the content of *Therapy*, which would be published in May, but in my solo event I gave a reading from the first chapter, based on personal experience, about Tubby undergoing an operation on his knee in a rundown Rummidge NHS hospital, because the private one he had expected to go to was closed at short notice for refurbishment. It was funny, and went down well with an audience who probably believed it was typical of the National Health Service, and could feel their own was superior. There was a party every evening to which we were invited, and late-night cabarets of a risqué character.

The British Council were hosting a big exhibition of books and posters called *The Art of Murder* during the Festival, a celebration of the crime novel, and had asked me if I would open it. I agreed, but began by admitting that I had no obvious qualifications to do so, because I have never written a novel about a murder, and seldom read murder mysteries by others. But crime fiction, especially the classic whodunnit, has a great attraction for narratologists because its rules and constraints are so identifiable, and I made some play with this in my opening speech:

> It has very ancient precursors, entwined in the deepest
> roots of human culture. The story of the Fall, for
> instance, inasmuch as it 'brought death into this world', in
> Milton's phrase, was a murder story. A child's retelling of
> the story in Genesis which I saw quoted in a newspaper
> once, recognised its affinity with the modern whodunnit.
> 'God said to Adam, "Did you eat the apple, Adam?" and
> Adam said "No, God." And God said to Eve, "Did you eat
> the apple, Eve?" And Eve said, "No, God." Then God said,
> "Well what are them two cores doing on the ground
> then?"'

I like that story, though I suspect it was invented by an adult.

At some point in the Writers' Week I met a former colleague at Birmingham University, Michael Wilding, who had been in the

English Department for a few years in the late sixties and early seventies. He was a scholarship boy who came from a working-class family in Worcestershire, read English at Oxford, got a First, and wrote a PhD on Milton. He took a job at the University of Sydney for a year, and came back to spend a couple more in the Birmingham English Department and the Shakespeare Institute, but he missed the relaxed and hedonistic atmosphere of Sydney and its environs and went back there permanently. He was now – in 1994 – a prominent figure in the Australian literary scene, as a writer and also publisher of books by himself and others, both fiction and non-fiction. His early novels and stories reminded me of West Coast American writing in the sixties and seventies, just as Sydney reminded me of San Francisco. He went on to write serious, scholarly non-fiction books as well as novels and short stories in a variety of modes and genres. His entry in Wikipedia reveals an astonishingly long and varied bibliography of his own publications. He is a greatly respected figure in Australia, but little known in his native country – which he returned to rarely and privately. In a Festschrift entitled *Running Wild* published in 2000 to mark his retirement, Michael recalled our meeting in Adelaide and a question I asked him on that occasion:

> David Lodge once asked me in perplexity, or maybe even in exasperation, 'So what are you? Are you an Australian writer or an English writer?' I suppose I wanted to be both. Or maybe neither. Transcending mere nationality. A citizen of the world. A writer . . . The writers I admired were many of them expatriates. Lawrence Durrell, Christopher Isherwood, Henry James, Joseph Conrad, D.H. Lawrence. It seemed the way to go. The future looked bleak in England. Three years at Oxford had made it clear to me that if you came from the working class, you were never going to be accepted by the ruling elite. And the ruling elite ran the cultural show.

Knowing that I would be returning home soon, Michael invited me to visit him in his own home on Scotland Island, off the coast near Sydney, and I accepted gladly. I took a train to a station called Pittwater, and then a one-man ferry to the island. Michael and his then wife Lyndy took me for a swim in the ocean and gave me lunch. Later in the day we sat on their deck overlooking the sea, and Lyndy brought us tea and biscuits. Michael laid out the latter on the balustrade of the veranda, and immediately a flock of white cockatoos with bright yellow crests swooped down from the surrounding trees and began to devour the biscuits. I shall never forget that startling moment. Apparently they arrived every day punctually at five o'clock. They were sulphur-crested cockatoos, Michael told me, when I wrote to him recently to check some details of this visit, and I asked him the same question as before. He replied, 'I'd like to think of myself as both an English and an Australian writer, but I'm not sure that's possible. I left England before establishing any identity there.' He also mentioned that he had to stop feeding the cockatoos because 'if they didn't get food they would start eating the deck and were doing massive damage.'

Whenever my thoughtstream touched on my brief visit to Australia subsequently, it triggered a recall of that sudden descent of the white cockatoos on to the balustrade of Michael Wilding's deck on Scotland Island, and by association the pleasantly relaxed day I spent with him and Lyndy. It epitomized for me the attractions of the Australian way of life. It was essentially a young person's idea of the good life. My elder son Stephen after graduation from university, like many of his peer group, travelled extensively around the world including Australia, but once returned to England he took advantage of the arrangement between the UK and Australia to allow young Brits to spend one year in Australia without formal emigration, and he returned from it to England reluctantly.

*

In the months following my return from Australia I went to some more locations where *Chuzzlewit* was being filmed, to keep in touch with the production team and the actors. But watching filming, with its frequent repeats of short takes, and – if you are the writer – listening to your own dialogue tested almost to destruction by repetition, is rather tedious, so I did not make many excursions of this kind. One of the most interesting, and comfortable, was a stay of several days in King's Lynn in Norfolk, which had been chosen as the location of the London scenes – London itself being impracticable for all outdoor filming because of traffic noise and other factors. The architecture of King's Lynn was right for the period of the story, and comparatively unspoiled by modernisation, but low in profile, so it was not possible to create the narrow, crooked alleys between tall, light-excluding tenements which Dickens describes; but few viewers would be troubled by that. Considering the limitations of his budget our designer, Gavin Davies, did wonders, there and elsewhere, with the look of the serial.

Filming ended in May, the editing process began, and gradually the serial began to take its final shape, always a thrilling experience after watching a lot of fragmentary 'rushes' and 'rough cuts'. How the last episode should end, however, was a matter of strong disagreement between myself and Pedr, which went down to the wire. The last act of Dickens' narrative is excessively long, and complicated by several subplots which I will not attempt to summarise. Earlier in the story old Martin, increasingly suspicious of Pecksniff's character, joined his household, pretending to be enfeebled in mind and body and in need of care, in order to observe his cousin's behaviour, and Pecksniff was only too happy to oblige, confident he would be repaid one day with a handsome legacy. But finally old Martin reveals his true, masterful self, and summons his relatives to a meeting where he rewards the good characters and punishes the bad. Pecksniff is denounced and chastised. Old Martin is reconciled with young Martin, and gives his blessing to the latter's marriage to Mary. Other unions between 'good' minor characters are in prospect, approved by old Martin.

It was our script editor, Nell Denton, who first threw out the suggestion of ending the very last episode with a double wedding, between young Martin and Mary, and between John Westlock (young Martin's predecessor as Pecksniff's apprentice, who had resigned in disgust with his employer) and Tom Pinch's sister Ruth, an engagement which in the novel she reveals to her brother at the wedding of young Martin and Mary. Nell's idea appealed to me partly because several of Shakespeare's 'happy endings' are associated with betrothals and nuptials. I added other couples to the procession from the church, inside which Tom Pinch is playing a wedding march on the organ. I thought it was a sequence over which the final credits might be scrolled. When I showed the script to Pedr however, he hated it. He thought it was a 'chocolate-boxy', feel-good ending which undermined the moral seriousness of the novel and especially the pathos of Tom Pinch's situation at the end of the story, denied the possibility of marrying Mary. Pedr wanted to end the last episode with Tom's speech to his sister Ruth, who empathises intensely with his disappointment: 'You think of me, Ruth, and it is very natural that you should, as if I was a character in a book; and you make a sort of poetical justice that I should, by some impossible means or other, come at last to marry the person I love. But there is a higher justice than the poetical kind my dear. I don't grieve for the impossible.' It is indeed a fine speech, and I had incorporated it into my script at an earlier point in the scene. It would have made a moving conclusion to the serial if Tom Pinch were the central character of the novel, but he is not. If there is one, it is old Martin.

'This book is not about marriage,' Pedr said to me more than once in the course of our discussion of the ending, and that is true. Indeed married life is conspicuous by its absence from the pages of Dickens' novel. As I worked on my adaptation it dawned on me what an extraordinary number of orphans, widows, widowers, bachelors and spinsters there are in it. Apart from the American episodes there is only one normal nuclear family depicted in the entire book, and that is the family of a minor character, Mr Mould the undertaker. Dickens invented the other incomplete, deviant, or divided family groups to communicate his vision of a society worm-eaten with selfishness. Old Martin himself is not blameless in this respect: a widower without living children, he buys himself a surrogate daughter from an orphanage and binds her to a degrading contract. These warped and exploitative relationships are superseded at the end of the story by the hopeful, loving marriages of the young couples.

There was much debate among the production team about the two rival endings, and in the end it was decided to film both and then make a decision. The disagreement between Pedr and me was leaked and caused a stir in the press, to the delight of the BBC's publicity department, for the story ran and ran in media coverage of the serial before and after its transmission began. In the end Pedr got his way by filming my ending with Tom Pinch bringing up the tail of the wedding procession and throwing confetti, while the organ he is supposed to be playing in the church is still on the soundtrack. This absurd twist was obviously unacceptable, and there was no time available to shoot the sequence again. But it seemed to me that to end the serial abruptly with a freeze frame after Tom's speech would leave our audience puzzled rather than satisfied, and that some gentler exit from the story was required. Dickens himself provided a coda in which he used the omniscient authorial voice to give his readers a comforting ending, summoning up a vision of Tom living happily in the home of Ruth and John Westlock:

Thy life is tranquil, calm and happy, Tom. In the soft
strain which ever and again comes stealing back upon the
ear, the memory of thine old love may find a voice
perhaps; but it is a pleasant, softened, whispering

memory, like that in which we sometimes hold the dead,
and does not pain or grieve thee, God be thanked.

To incorporate this vision, which is developed at some length in extravagantly religiose diction, into our serial, was out of the question; but I suggested to Pedr that we might gesture towards it by having a final shot of Tom, seen from behind, arm in arm between Ruth and John Westlock as they walk out of the church-yard into their future together. There was an archway in place in the location which would have provided a very effective frame for such a conclusion. Pedr seemed quite taken with this idea, and agreed to think about it. But it turned out that there was no time available to film it.

5

It was evident before it was broadcast that *Chuzzlewit* was going to be a success. The first independent and unprompted indication was a letter I received early in September from Professor Michael Slater of Birkbeck College in the University of London, who had been shown a video when participating in a BBC educational programme about Dickens. He wrote, 'I would like to congratulate you on your very deftly done TV adaptation of *Chuzzlewit*... I really admired the cunning of it, a wonderful example of a loose baggy monster transformed into a shapely organism.' I believed that our version of Dickens' novel would appeal to the average viewer, but to have this endorsement from one of the most distinguished Dickens scholars in the world was immensely reassuring. His only criticisms of the production were about the casting of young Martin and a few minor parts.

In October there was a screening of the long first episode at the BAFTA headquarters in Piccadilly. It looked terrific on the big screen, enhanced by the music composed by Geoffrey Burgon, who had won awards for his contributions to TV serials such as *Brideshead Revisited* and *Tinker Tailor Soldier Spy*. I had been listening to his music for *Chuzzlewit* on a cassette at home and in my car for weeks, never tiring of it. He wrote a lovely letter to me, praising the adaptation and saying, 'It was a pleasure to work on the series as there were so many opportunities to write all sorts of dramatic, dark, grotesque, comic, romantic etc. music.' The audience at the screening, made up of BBC staff, journalists, people in show business and members of our cast and production team, applauded warmly at the end. Among several personal friends at the reception afterwards were Michael Frayn and his wife Claire Tomalin. I was pleased when Michael complimented me on the screenplay, as I had long admired his own writing for stage, film and television. Later Claire sent me an insightful letter which displayed complete familiarity with the novel and awareness of the challenges it presented for adaptation. Perhaps she had recently reread it in preparation for her acclaimed biography of Dickens, published in 2011.

The first episode was broadcast on Monday the 7th of November, which seemed perverse scheduling to most of us who were involved in the production, firstly because Sunday is generally regarded as the best day of the week to air a classic serial, and secondly because it put us in direct competition with the detective series *Cracker* on ITV, starring the immensely popular actor Robbie Coltrane. The viewing figures were satisfactory however, and the press reviews predominantly favourable. Even the late A.A. Gill, television critic of the *Sunday Times*, notorious for his witty demolition of programmes which displeased him, and by his own confession prejudiced against adaptations of classic novels – even *he* capitulated to the appeal of *Chuzzlewit*, blessed it for getting him through a bout of flu, and gave it a rave review. On the 18th of November, the London *Evening Standard* devoted the final paragraph of its editorial leader to our programme:

> *Martin Chuzzlewit* is a new delight for the winter months amid the rotten leaves of television. Paul Scofield is quite splendid in the title role but Tom Wilkinson's Seth Pecksniff is a new monument to comic, blustering humbug. Watching his entry to a room – 'May I enter this bower of bliss?' – some viewers may have felt Mr Pecksniff bore a strong resemblance to a character off last night's news.

This was a reference to the Conservative cabinet minister David Mellor, who had been forced to resign from office because of a much-publicised sex scandal. I was amused by the writer's choice of quotation, words which are not in Dickens' text but were written by me. I had borrowed the phrase 'bower of bliss' (referring to the parlour occupied by Pecksniff's daughters at Todgers's) from Edmund Spenser's epic poem, *The Faerie Queene.*

Altogether I had far more attention in the press about *Chuzzlewit*, in the form of reviews, featured interviews and articles, many of them concentrating on my dispute with Pedr over the ending, and often requiring published corrections by me, than I ever received before or since for any of my novels. If fame is measured by newspaper column inches, rather than their content, this was probably my finest hour. I sent Dad some of the press cuttings, which added to his intense enjoyment of the serial. He had been a devoted reader of Dickens since childhood, and after watching the first episode he wrote: 'You have every reason to be proud of your efforts. The way everything moved along was marvellous, and with such a magnificent cast the inspiration was already there ... Nobody in the world but Scofield would do for his part obviously. Magnificent. And the casting for Tom Pinch was an undoubted triumph. Pity about the bald head. I remember trying to get you into Dickens when you were about 13 but you were very sceptical and you used to murmur to mother, "Here we go again – Saint Dickens". You won't remember it but I assure you it's true.' He was right: I didn't remember it. It was teaching Dickens much later that belatedly showed me his genius.

Birmingham took some local pride and considerable interest in *Chuzzlewit*, produced at the BBC's Pebble Mill studios. The serial was celebrated on the 20th of November by a performance of Geoffrey Burgon's *Chuzzlewit Suite* by the City of Birmingham Symphony Orchestra, billed as a 'world premiere' in the local evening paper. The suite formed the second half of a concert in the magnificent Symphony Hall opened a few years previously in the city centre, largely thanks to the dynamic leadership of Sir Simon Rattle, the CBSO's Music Director since 1980. We didn't have him as conductor for our event, but Barry Wordsworth performed the task admirably, and it was wonderful to hear the music in an auditorium with state-of-the-art acoustics. I introduced the session standing at the front of the stage and Philip Franks read some passages from the novel between the movements of the suite.

When *Chuzzlewit* was about to begin transmission the *Radio Times* had a teaser headline on its cover, '*How the Dickens do you follow* **MIDDLEMARCH**?' followed in smaller type by: 'Why BBC2 has great expectations for *Martin Chuzzlewit*, starting Monday.' *Middlemarch* had been adapted by Andrew Davies, and was well received when it was broadcast earlier in the year. I wrote to an American friend at that time: 'The BBC have been transmitting *Middlemarch* here in the last six weeks, with unprecedented media coverage – a kind of *Middlemarch* mania seems to be sweeping the country.' There was a strange symmetry between these two serial adaptations of classic Victorian novels – both commissioned by the BBC, both written by graduates of the UCL English Department, both of whom belonged to the same regular writers' lunch group. The parallels went further: Andrew Davies had serious disagreements about the screenplay of *Middlemarch* with his director, Anthony Page, as I did with Pedr. In fact, their

61

relations were so strained that all the rewrites were negotiated by the two producers.

The serial ended its run a few weeks before Christmas. I am not usually a fan of this commercialised ritual, but for once I really enjoyed exchanging Christmas cards because the ones I received invariably contained messages expressing the senders' great enjoyment of *Chuzzlewit*. In the first week of the New Year I received a letter congratulating me on the adaptation from John Birt, then Director General of the BBC, and later another from the Chairman of the BBC's Board of Governors, Marmaduke Hussey, congratulating us on winning the Sanyo trophy for BBC Programme of the Year at an occasion called the 1995 TRIC Awards, which I had never heard of before. His letter had a handwritten postscript: 'You've brought great credit to us. We bask in your glory.'

I was pleased to have their approval, though disappointed in March that *Chuzzlewit* was not one of the nominations for Best TV Drama Serial in the annual BAFTA awards. Our actors, however, made a brilliant showing on that occasion, as they deserved. Unprecedentedly, three out of the four nominations for Best Actor in television drama that year were chosen from the same production: they were Tom Wilkinson, Paul Scofield and Pete Postlethwaite. This award, unlike the others for acting, was decided by the popular vote of viewers, and predictably it went to Robbie Coltrane, but Tom Wilkinson got his rightful due with the Royal Television Society's Best Actor award a few months later. I read a newspaper interview with him at this time in which he revealed that he had never read *Martin Chuzzlewit*. This absolutely astonished me, because he seemed to have achieved such a total identification with Dickens' character. That he managed this feat without recourse to the book said something for the screenplay, I thought; but it was also the mark of a great actor.

I turned sixty on the 28th of January 1995, and had arranged to celebrate it with a big dinner for family and friends. The date conveniently fell on a Saturday, allowing those who lived far away to stay overnight at a hotel owned by neighbours of ours who offered them a discount. I had planned it months in advance, and chose for the venue a restaurant called Sloans, situated in a quiet square near our house, which offered something like fine dining years before that phrase was common usage in Birmingham. I took Gore Vidal there after interviewing him on stage at the Midlands Arts Centre some years earlier, and he commended the duck with blackcurrant sauce. Some time in the autumn of 1994, I went to the restaurant to make a booking but I was dismayed to find it closed, and evidence that the interior was being extensively remodelled and the restaurant renamed Sloans Brasserie. When I managed to speak to the couple who were the new proprietors they were very pleasant, welcomed my interest, and promised that the transformation of the interior would be completed well before the end of January. I decided that the dining area they were creating would be more suitable for the large party I envisaged, and made a reservation. From time to time I would peep through the windows of the restaurant to monitor progress. When it opened for business, just about in time to settle my nerves, Mary and I had a meal there and were well pleased.

Then, to my dismay, a few weeks before the dinner a disparaging review of the restaurant appeared in the colour supplement of a Sunday paper – I can't remember which one, because I tore it up and threw it away. It was written in the patronising style with which London columnists tended in those days to denigrate provincial culture, Birmingham's in particular, on the rare occasions when they deigned to visit the city. I was sure that a number of my guests would have seen the review and be bracing themselves for a dreary meal, and this obsessed and depressed me right up to the event itself, which was in fact a great success.

I particularly cherished a thank you letter written by my agent's wife, Marian Shaw, who knew of my anxiety beforehand: 'It was a really lovely evening for us. I was delighted to be seated between Christopher and his Grandad (I worked out there is a sixty year gap between them, so sixty was definitely the magic number). I really enjoyed getting to know them both and I think they're *great* people. Christopher's witty interjections were amazing. The happy atmosphere, the informal and varied speeches, made it an excellent evening, along with the really delicious food and wine. Bad reviews clearly need to be put to the test.' It is pleasant to be reminded of what a lively, articulate young man our Down's son Chris was at this stage of his life, aged twenty-nine. Now in his fifties, he is less talkative, though he still surprises us occasionally with a sophisticated word or phrase.

6

Chuzzlewit was broadcast in America in March 1995 by PBS, the public service channel maintained by voluntary subscriptions, and was very well received there, to judge by the letters of friends who watched it. It continues to be enjoyed around the world on the BBC's DVD and through 'secondary use' in foreign countries. But now my thoughts were focussed on the forthcoming publication of *Therapy*. I had finished this novel in the summer of 1994, and delivered it to Secker & Warburg, via Mike Shaw, in August. As was my usual practice, I had not shown any of it previously to the key people concerned, and as always there was some suspense for me as well as for them at this moment. I did not doubt that they would accept the book – but would they love it? Happily they did. Mike sent me a wonderful letter, revealing incidentally that he had walked a large part of the Camino with a group of friends in the past; Tom Rosenthal left a rhapsodic message on my answerphone, and John Blackwell wrote: 'It's an astoundingly brave book – technically, socially, emotionally, politically, and is it I wonder, a first? (Polyphonic first-person narrative with a single narrator – I can't recall any worthwhile precedent.)' A contract was drawn up, and publication planned for the spring of the following year.

Soon a good deal of thought was given in-house to the design of the jacket, which has a significant influence on the success of a new book – on orders from booksellers in the run-up to publication, as well as on the impulses of bookshop browsers. It is an aspect of book production in which I have always taken a keen interest, and by chance I was able to come up with a design which pleased everyone concerned. In July the Tate Gallery (now known as Tate Britain) opened a retrospective exhibition of the work of R.B. Kitaj, an American artist of mixed Hungarian and Jewish descent who had worked in London for many years and was associated with artists such as Frank Auerbach, Leon Kossoff, Francis Bacon and Lucian Freud. His own work was varied in subject matter and style, full of political and literary references and commentary. I wasn't then familiar with Kitaj's paintings, but I loved the huge tapestry which he designed, commissioned by the new British Library to hang in its entrance hall. Enigmatically entitled *If Not, Not*, it struck me as an updated visual equivalent of Eliot's *The Waste Land*, a montage of fragmentary images evoking the chaos and violence of twentieth-century history, while possessing a paradoxical beauty.

The retrospective at the Tate was however savagely attacked by a number of influential London art critics, who accused Kitaj of trying to give poorly executed paintings a spurious importance by incorporating pretentious cultural references. There was a whiff of anti-intellectual chauvinism about this reaction, and perhaps anti-semitism too – Kitaj certainly thought so – which made me determined to see the exhibition for myself. I left it late, and didn't get to the Tate until two days before the exhibition was to close. I was fascinated by the range and variety of the work on show and took my time going round the exhibition, until I came to the last room, a small one. I went in to find the walls hung with a series of recent oil paintings in matching frames, illustrating ailments of middle-aged men in an Expressionist style, as if created by a pupil of Munch who had developed a sense of humour. They had titles: *Bad Back*, *Bad Neck*, *Bad Foot*, *Bad Arm* . . . Would there be a knee, I wondered, as I moved slowly from one picture to the next, dreading disappointment. There *had* to be, surely? And there was! The last painting was entitled *Bad Knee*.

It depicted a man, tall and thin, in profile, trudging along a paved road with a vague landscape in the background. His shoulders were hunched and his head bowed as he stared at the ground before him, and with one hand he clutched his right knee, which was surrounded by a red aura of pain. It was the perfect cover image for *Therapy*. The man not only had a bad knee, he also looked like a pilgrim on the Camino, with a sun hat on his head, and something like a small rucksack on his back. I bought a postcard reproduction of the painting and took it straight to Secker's offices, where it was acclaimed by everyone who had read the novel. An application for permission to reproduce the painting on the jacket for *Therapy* was made to Kitaj through his agents, Marlborough Galleries. He agreed promptly and generously waived a fee, asking only for free copies of the book to give to his friends. By this time he had returned to America, disgusted by the hostile criticism of his work in London, and devastated by the sudden death of his beautiful and beloved wife from an aneurism in the brain, which he attributed (probably wrongly, but understandably) to the stress she had shared with him at the reception of his retrospective.

In addition, I took away with me from that exhibition the Tate's poster for the event. It featured a painting by Kitaj called *Cecil Court*, the name of a pedestrian passage very near my London flat, through which I often take a short cut. It is lined with small shops selling second-hand books and rare modern first editions, antique bric-a-brac, old maps and prints, and other collectibles. Kitaj's painting depicts the court from an elevated position, with himself lying on a couch across the entrance, dreaming of exotically dressed figures hovering there and outside the shopfronts, who are characters derived from traditional Jewish theatre. I had this poster framed, and it hangs on the wall of my flat's living room. I corresponded with Kitaj occasionally, and he told me that when he lived in London he had a friend who lived in Cecil Court whom he frequently visited. When Kitaj received his finished copies of the novel some six months later he was delighted, and wrote from Los Angeles: 'I just *love* the look of your new book with Bad Knee on it. Someone did a terrific design of the cover. Please pass this well-deserved plaudit to your art department.' I was glad to do so, and pleased that he liked the cover, because in due course my American publisher, Viking, adopted the same image for the cover of its own edition.

Therapy was published on Monday the 1st of May, 1995. As I described in *Writer's Luck*, this was a period when publishers spent lavishly on publicity for books they were strongly committed to, so there was a big launch party at Groucho's, a venue I suggested because Tubby is a member and occasionally meets his agent Jake there for lunch. 'It's his kind of place,' he writes in his journal, 'Everybody is there to see and be seen without letting on . . . There's a special kind of glance that *habitués* have perfected I call the Groucho Fast Pan, which consists in sweeping the room with your eyes very rapidly under half-lowered lids, checking for the presence of celebrities, while laughing like a drain at something your companion has said, whether it's funny or not.' It was a big, very enjoyable party, followed by a dinner at Au Jardin des Gourmets in Soho.

As always, I was braced for the reviews, a prospect which I think most novelists regard with a mixture of hope and apprehension, and some avoid by not reading them at all (or claiming not to).[1] Novelists, like all professional artists, are very sensitive to

[1] I have a cartoon by the *Guardian's* Biff permanently pinned to the corkboard in my study which portrays a writer and his wife at breakfast. The writer says, 'I make it a principle never to read reviews of my own work,' and the wife says from behind her newspaper, 'Just as well, really – There aren't any.'

criticism because they are continually and publicly exposed to it. Works of art in any medium are gratuitous acts by the maker – the world could get on with its business perfectly well without this or that one, and their justification is that they please. The more successful you are in this respect, the greater is the pressure of readers' expectations, and the more anxious therefore the writer becomes about the reception of a new work. Reviews are not the only indicators, but they are the first. Sales and word of mouth come later. Much depends of course on the status of the reviewer. John Mortimer's review of *Therapy* was the first to appear, on the front of the Books section in *The Sunday Times*, and was what the trade call 'a good selling review', not only because he said positive things about the novel but also because he was so well known as creator of *Rumpole of the Bailey*, and generally liked. Secker had arranged a series of bookshop signings for me, and my first customer in Hatchards on the following day was a smiling middle-aged woman who announced, 'I'm married to Tubby Passmore.' She had read Mortimer's review, and wanted a signed copy of *Therapy* for her husband, who she said was a balding depressive with a bad knee.

Therapy had widespread review coverage over the next few weeks, with the usual mixture of praise and complaint, but it was mainly favourable. I particularly appreciated reviews by Anita Brookner in the *Spectator*, Valentine Cunningham in the *Observer*, and Carol Angier in the *New Statesman*, who wrote: '*Therapy* is a perfect Lodge trick. It seems absolutely modern – but is in fact ancient, or timeless; it seems a comedy – but is about the stuff of tragedy: love and betrayal, good and evil, guilt and sin.'

Of course, there were dissenters. David Sexton, who had led the attack on *Paradise News*, reviewed *Therapy* more temperately in the *Guardian*, but found nothing in it to praise and managed to make it seem dull. Perhaps he was wrong-footed by the fact that it was completely different in form and content from any previous novel of mine, so he could not make his usual complaint of formulaic writing. The editor responsible for commissioning fiction reviews in the *Guardian* at this time was James Wood, a close friend of David Sexton. They had read English at Cambridge together, and came down from the University determined to shake up the metropolitan literary scene, and in particular to denounce the state of contemporary British literary fiction. I was on their hit list, but in good company. In 1994 Wood had been one of the judges for the Booker Prize, and he gave the after-dinner speech normally given by the chairperson. (How did he manage that, one wondered.)The next day's *Guardian* reported that in the course of it he declared, 'Julian Barnes, William Boyd and David Lodge are not serious novelists, and it is the duty of criticism to say so.' The arrogance and pomposity of this statement, especially when delivered in that context, must have made his fellow judges cringe. They had previously been disconcerted by Wood when he listened silently for some time to their private discussion of a longlisted novel by Claire Messud before revealing that she was his wife, after which he was required to leave the room when her book was discussed. Wood soon recruited another young reviewer for the *Guardian*, Philip Hensher, a novelist and critic who specialised in witty hatchet jobs, for which Jim Crace coined a new verb, expressing relief to me that, so far, he hadn't been 'henshered'. Neither had I, but Hensher's cruel review of Malcolm Bradbury's *To the Hermitage*, published in the *Guardian* in the summer of 2000, greatly increased the misery of the last year of my friend's life. Hensher wouldn't have been aware that Malcolm was seriously ill because it was kept secret, and may have regretted writing the review later. He has mellowed as a critic in middle age.

In 1995 James Wood moved to America and became a senior editor at *The New Republic* in Washington DC. For some years previously I had enjoyed a happy relationship with the Literary Editor there, who admired my work and invited me to review occasionally for the magazine. The reviews of my own books which she published were always fair, until Wood displaced her.

From that time until he left the magazine in 2007 I did not receive a single favourable review in it. In 2004 he himself contributed a review of *Author, Author*, my novel about Henry James, which a concerned American friend described in a letter as 'vitriolic'. I was grateful for the warning. I didn't want to see vitriol poured over a book of mine of which I am particularly proud, so I never read Wood's review. My American publishers tactfully omitted it from the batch they sent me, and I didn't seek it out. In that same year Wood published his own first novel, portentously entitled *The Book Against God*. It was not well received and he didn't publish another until fourteen years later. It was not noticeably more successful.

In 2007 Wood moved to New York, joined the staff of the *New Yorker* and began to write reviews and essays for it, and other prestigious journals. In 2014 he became 'Professor of the Practice of Literary Criticism' at Harvard University, a title no doubt chosen by him. He has been described as the best critic currently writing in English, admired by writers such as Martin Amis and Zadie Smith. He is certainly clever, well educated and widely read, and has a facility for flowery writing, but his kind of criticism cannot be taught because it has no methodological basis. It is intuitive, personal, and exhibitionist – an updated version of the belletrist, musing-in-the-library style that characterised British literary criticism in the late-nineteenth century and early-twentieth century, before the advent of the English and American New Criticism in the 1920s and later of structuralism and poststructuralism. He smothers the work under examination with his own ornate rhetoric and a tissue of allusions to other texts and authors, until it is almost unrecognisable, and only he can elucidate it. This style made a refreshing change from much of the dry-as-dust criticism written under the influence of Theory at this period, which explains Wood's popularity with readers bored to death by it, but his own practice is useless as a model for young aspiring critics.

*

Therapy went into the *Sunday Times* bestseller list at number 3 in the week after publication, and figured somewhere in the top 10 throughout the rest of the year. This was partly due to the efforts of Sarah Smythe, my new publicist at Secker, who later became Director of the Cheltenham Literary Festival. She arranged press interviews before publication with several national newspapers and presented me with a formidable list of future engagements in the coming weeks and months, events at festivals and bookshops in Brighton, Bath, Birmingham, Hay, Canterbury, Blackheath, Manchester and Dublin. I was also booked to speak at the Dartington Festival in September and the Cheltenham Festival in October. On these occasions authors signed books afterwards, and usually someone I knew, a former student or friend, was in the line. Mary helped me by getting the punters to write their names on a piece of paper if they wanted an inscription, since my deafness could be a problem. This signing ritual epitomised the change that had taken place in literary publishing, requiring the author to take part in the marketing of his or her book. I was happy to do it, but it could be an uncomfortable experience for other writers whose queues were short or non-existent.

Therapy was published in America in July '95 and, James Wood aside, got excellent reviews, but the one that gave me most pleasure was by the novelist Jane Smiley in the *Los Angeles Times*, which was more like an essay than a review. She surveyed my career as a novelist, making the kind of observations that publishers love to quote, and authors cherish. Its opening paragraph, in which she declared that I was 'one of the few writers whose roster of novels I have read in its entirety,' as well as being a very gratifying surprise, made me guiltily aware that I had not got around to reading any of hers, including *A Thousand Acres*, for which she won a Pulitzer Prize in 1992. I knew that it was a very long book, a modern reworking of the plot of *King Lear* about a farmer and his three daughters on their farm in Iowa, and that I couldn't possibly read it or any other of her novels, which tended to be long, in time to include some appropriate complimentary remarks in a letter thanking Jane Smiley for her generous review. I therefore post-poned the task, and eventually forgot about it. But later I read her novel, *Moo*, a satirical account of a year in the life of an American mid-western university, and was so impressed that I revived my original impulse to write to her, as follows:

> Dear Jane Smiley,
> I meant to write and thank you for the wonderful review of *Therapy* that you wrote for the *LA Times* last year, but was inhibited by the shaming fact that I had not read any of your books, while you had paid me the ultimate compliment of reading all of mine. Well, I have redressed the balance to a small extent, having recently read *Moo*, which I hugely enjoyed and admired. I was particularly impressed by the multiplicity of characters, all so convincingly portrayed, and the interdisciplinary scope of the book. Most campus novels, including my own, ignore the sciences because the writers, like me, don't know enough about science to do otherwise.
> With best wishes, David Lodge

Jane replied promptly and warmly, and so began a very rewarding friendship conducted mainly by correspondence, with meetings at long intervals in England when literary business brought her there. We must have been an odd couple to behold on these occa-sions because Jane is about six foot six in height, and I am just under five foot eight. She is a remarkable person in many respects: good-looking, clever, a professor of English Literature and Crea-tive Writing, as well as the owner of a ranch where she breeds and rides horses. She has written a score of novels, mostly long ones, and it was not surprising to discover that she is devoted to English nineteenth-century fiction, especially Dickens and Trollope. She put me on to the first two novels Trollope wrote, drawing on his experience as a surveyor of Post Offices in Ireland in the 1840s, *The Macdermots of Ballycloran* (1847) and *The Kellys and the O'Kellys* (1848). They were a revelation to me, the second one in particular. The books for which Trollope is best known are all about the English middle and upper classes, but these early novels show he closely observed Irish manners and speech of *all* classes, and was able to represent them to excellent effect in fiction.

Jane also prompted me to read his very late book, *The Fixed Period*, generally ignored or deplored by Trollope fans. It is a futuristic novel written in 1880 but set in 1980, about a small British island colony in the antipodes whose parliament declares independence and votes to introduce compulsory euthanasia for every citizen after a fixed period of life (sixty-seven and a half years), in order to increase the prosperity of the population by eliminating unproductive members, while at the same time relieving the latter of the inevitable afflictions of old age. I was fascinated by the relevance of this fable to our own society's current preoccupation with the problems created by longevity, especially the increasing number of people afflicted by dementia. It prompted me to write a short article about *The Fixed Period* for the *Guardian Review*, and in preparing this I discovered from his letters that Trollope himself had a horror of succumbing to dementia, though he didn't use that word. At the beginning of November 1882, the year in which *The Fixed Period* was published, he suffered a severe stroke, which paralysed his right side and deprived him of speech, but this fate, almost as bad as what he had feared, was mercifully brief. He died in a nursing home on the 6th of December, five months short of his sixty-eighth birthday, almost exactly the 'fixed period' of his novel.

In September '95 I received a letter from the Writers' Guild, a trade union open to writers in all forms and genres, to say that *Martin*

Chuzzlewit had been nominated for Best Television Drama Serial in the Guild's annual awards, and *Therapy* for Best Novel. I was invited with Mary to attend the awards dinner at the Intercontinental hotel in London in October. The first nomination was a surprise, because it came nearly a year after *Chuzzlewit* had been first shown on television; but having been disappointed that it did not feature in the BAFTA awards, I was delighted by this unexpected tribute. Likewise, the shortlisting of *Therapy* was some compensation for being passed over by the Booker judges. The other nomination for the Guild's Best Novel was Nick Hornby's *High Fidelity*, which I soon read, and was fascinated to discover that the story began with the hero trying to trace a former girlfriend, like Tubby Passmore in the last part of my own novel.

I was not a member of the Guild, having been for many years a member of the Society of Authors, but all professional writers are eligible for its awards. No money is attached to them – it is simply an honour to receive such a tribute from one's peers. Being nominated in two different categories, with their different panels of judges, was gratifying in one respect, but worrying in another. To win in both would be great, but to be unsuccessful in both would be depressing. The Best Novel award was presented first, to Nick Hornby. The other work nominated for Best TV Drama Serial was *Taking Over The Asylum*, a lively Scottish production about the internal radio station of a psychiatric hospital, which I had enjoyed watching. The judges gave the award to *Martin Chuzzlewit*, and with great relief I stepped up to the platform to receive some record of the award to hang on the wall of my study, and to shake the hand of Alan Plater. He was one of the most distinguished members of the Guild, a prolific writer of screenplays, stage plays and novels, including *Fortunes of War*, his brilliant TV adaptation of Olivia Manning's *Balkan Trilogy* for the BBC in 1987, which had greatly impressed me.

Leah Schmidt attended the event. Though she had drawn up the contract for my screenplay of *Martin Chuzzlewit*, she was not a Dickens fan – in fact the reverse – and did not pretend to have loved the series. But she did take pleasure in my contribution to its success. 'Well, now you'll be able to adapt any novel you like,' she said with a smile, when I came up to her at the end of the presentations. That was overstated, but not absurdly so. I had written only two screenplays for television which had actually been produced and broadcast, but both *Nice Work* and *Chuzzlewit* had been hugely successful, so were likely to attract further commissions of the same kind. But in fact, I never obtained even one, for several reasons.

If Chris Parr had remained Head of Drama at BBC Pebble Mill I'm sure he would have tried to persuade me to collaborate with him again on a major serial, and probably I would have agreed, but he left the BBC's employ not long after *Chuzzlewit* to work with another television company, and a few years later he and his wife Ann Devlin returned to live in Northern Ireland. The adaptation projects that were occasionally offered to me after *Chuzzlewit* did not appeal, though one of them gave me an idea for a new novel, *Author, Author*, published in 2004. I regarded myself as primarily a novelist, and I was interested in adapting my own novels for television or, better still, feature films, rather than adapting the work of other writers. I continued to publish a new novel at intervals of four or five years, and was always ready to consider propositions to adapt one of them for film or TV. I should have been mindful of the apothegm, '*Be careful what you wish for.*'

7

There are basically two ways in which feature films based on books are produced: either by a big company with enough money at its disposal to cover the entire cost, from obtaining the rights to releasing the finished film; or by a smaller independent company which will begin by taking out an option on the rights in the book, preventing any other company making a film of it, and then looking to various sources to finance the different stages of production: the writing (and rewriting) of the screenplay, appointment of a director, casting of actors, scouting for locations, etc. etc. This is sometimes called 'Development Hell', because it consumes an enormous amount of time and energy for those involved and often ends with nothing achieved.

I had had a little experience of this process in the past, with projects which quickly evaporated. My first real immersion in it started a few months after the publication of *Therapy*, when I was contacted by Stephen Evans, a producer who was interested in making a feature film of my novel. I said I would be agreeable provided I could write the screenplay. I thought this was the best way to ensure that the film would be faithful to the essential elements of the book. I was well aware that no film can include all the dense detail of a novel, and that adaptation always demands a great deal of condensation, but if the filmmaker has a completely free hand the finished product can be almost unrecognisable from its source. Stephen had watched and approved my adaptations of *Nice Work* and *Chuzzlewit*, and accepted this condition.

He took me to lunch at his dining club, and we had an amicable and promising conversation. He told me he had been a stockbroker originally, but moved into film production as co-chairman of Renaissance Films, a respected company which specialised in films with a literary source, such as Kenneth Branagh's *Henry V* and an adaptation of Vladimir Nabokov's novel, *The Luzhin Defence*. Henry James' novel *The Wings of the Dove* was in Stephen's plans for the future. I found his literary taste reassuring and we got on very well. By the time we left the dining club Stephen had agreed to approach Leah Schmidt to obtain the rights in *Therapy* and negoti- ate a contract for me to write the screenplay. I was elated, and still more so when Leah agreed a contract with Stephen for a substantial fee. It was one I would fully earn, for the script went through seven drafts, written and rewritten over several years.

During the same period I was also writing or preparing to write two new novels. *Thinks . . .* , published in 2001 and *Author, Author*, published in 2004. That was not such a big workload to combine with the development of *Therapy* as it might seem, because there is little actual text in a film script, and most of the work involves selecting, cutting, joining up and revising the essen- tial elements of the story, taking into account the opinions and interventions of various people who have a role in the produc- tion. Most of the printed matter generated by a film in develop- ment consists of letters, emails and faxes between these people, and much of the time devoted to the project is taken up with their phone calls and meetings with each other.

Novelists tend to be solitary, introspective types, jealously guarding their ideas for and progress with new work until it is finished. The production of films and stage plays however is a collective and collaborative process, and people employed in those areas like to work with other people they know and trust. I identified the same instinct in myself. In conversation with Stephen about a possible director for the film I thought immediately of Mike Ockrent, who had been so helpful to me in the writing and rewriting of my first play *The Writing Game*. He was known chiefly as a successful director of plays by some of Britain's top playwrights and also admired for his acclaimed revivals of classic musicals. Always ambitious to extend his range, he had turned lately to directing films, and one I had seen in 1990, *Dancin' Thru The Dark*, had impressed me with its mastery of the medium, considering how recently he had taken it up, so I proposed him as the director of *Therapy*. Stephen was taken with the idea and consulted others at Renaissance who agreed. Mike was attached to the project, though his contribution would not be needed immediately, so he was free to go to America to fulfil a directing commitment. Alas, he became seriously ill there, was hospitalised and diagnosed as suffering from leukaemia, which proved to be incurable. He died in New York in 1999, at the age of fifty-three, to the dismay and great distress of his family, friends, and everybody who knew him and had worked with him – above all, his lovely and talented wife and collaborator, the choreographer Susan Stroman. He was one of the friendliest, cleverest and most genuinely kind individuals I had met in the world of show business, and I was devastated by his death. It was both a personal loss and a damaging one to the development of the film we had begun to work on together.

After Mike's death, I suggested that David Thacker might replace him as director. He had had a distinguished career in the theatre, winning many awards for his productions of classic and modern plays, but like several other established theatre directors, he had worked his way into television in middle life to learn the craft of filming with the BBC. By now he had directed many well-received films both classic and modern for the Beeb. His CV displayed a career of extraordinary scope and distinction, from an Olivier award for his production of Shakespeare's *Pericles*, to a highly praised new film for the BBC about the Miners' Strike of 1972. Recalling that it was his enthusiasm for *Therapy*, conveyed to me in a fan letter soon after it was published, that first brought us together, I thought he would be an ideal director for the film, and Stephen Evans was of my opinion, though he did not immediately draw up an agreement to that effect.

When I submitted my first draft screenplay Stephen professed to be delighted, but the development of the film progressed at a painfully slow pace. David introduced his favoured casting agent, Jill Trevillick to me. She loved the script and the three of us drew up a suggested cast list which we submitted to Stephen. It included Ken Stott or Alfred Molina for Tubby, Miranda Richardson or Lindsay Duncan for his wife Sally, Emma Thompson for the adult Maureen (formerly his teenage sweetheart) and Tom Wilkinson for her husband, Bede. I suggested Ardal O'Hanlon for the Catholic curate in the teenage flashback sequence set in and around the youth club where Tubby's relationship with the young Maureen began. Ardal is a stand-up comedian and actor, famous for his performance as the gormless Father Dougal McGuire in the popular Irish TV sitcom *Father Ted*. He also happens to be the son of one of Mary's Irish cousins.

None of these excellent actors was eventually cast in those roles. In fact, no casting director had been attached to the film by the autumn of 2000, and even the basic agreement for Renaissance to make the film had not been signed. David Thacker and I were exasperated by Stephen Evans' indecisiveness. I wrote to Leah at this point:

I believe he doesn't want to make this movie in case it fails; but on the other hand, he doesn't want to NOT make the movie, in case someone else makes it and it succeeds. His behaviour can only be explained as designed, consciously or unconsciously, to prevent the film being made while keeping alive the hypothetical possibility of making it.

We began to think of approaching other producers, and David came up with the name Trudie Styler. It was not familiar to me, which shows that I did not keep up with the lives of 'celebrities', for she was famous to many as the wife of Sting, a.k.a. Gordon Matthew Thomas Sumner, a vocalist with the rock band *Police*, who began a successful solo career in 1985. David told me that he had known Trudie well as an actress when they were both young, and he still kept in touch with her. She and Sting had prospered, and now lived in high style, with homes in England, Italy and New York, jetting to and fro between these locations, while looking after the Rainforest Foundation Fund, an organisation they founded to protect rainforests and their indigenous peoples. Shortly before the film of *Therapy* was being developed, Trudie had founded her own production company in London called Xingu which produced films, including Guy Ritchie's successful *Lock, Stock and Two Smoking Barrels*. David suggested we should ask Trudie if she was interested in getting involved in our film. I agreed, and she was. She was also interested in having a small part in it if possible, as she missed the buzz of acting. Her energy and appetite for new projects seemed unlimited.

She took me to lunch at a fashionable restaurant in West London (Harold Pinter was at the next table) and revealed that she was born and brought up in Bromsgrove, near Birmingham, the daughter of a farmer and a factory worker. Her rise to fame and fortune seemed all the more remarkable. She spoke candidly and from experience of the difficulties of making films with a small independent company, and I was favourably impressed. Later I visited her London headquarters: a large town house in the St

James's area, not far from Buckingham Palace, and one of the most prestigious addresses in London. Each floor was dedicated to one of Trudie's enterprises, and at the top was a large private apartment for the family. A regiment of servants, secretaries and other helpers serviced the building and its occupants.

8

In July 1995 my editor Geoff Mulligan phoned to tell me that *Therapy* had won the award for Best Novel in the so-called 'Eurasian region' of the Commonwealth Writers' Prize – news that was all the more welcome because the novel had so far received no such recognition from any other body. Established by the Commonwealth Foundation in 1987, this prize was awarded annually for the best novel by a citizen of a Commonwealth country in one of four 'regions': Africa; Caribbean and Canada; South East Asia and South Pacific; and South Asia and Europe (including the UK) which was called 'Eurasia'. The prize for the winner was £10,000 and a private audience with the Queen at Buckingham Palace. The sum of £1000 was awarded for the Best Novels in each region, and all of those went forward to the final judgement for the main prize. I was glad when I learned that *Therapy* had won at the first stage against three novels shortlisted for the previous year's Booker Prize, for which *Therapy* hadn't even been longlisted, confirming my belief that the results of such competitions are largely determined by the organisers' initial choice of the judges, with their different tastes and prejudices.

The final judging process and award ceremony of this prize took place in a different Commonwealth city each year, to which all the candidates were invited as guests for one week, and this year the venue was Harare, capital of Zimbabwe. I had never been further south in Africa than Morocco, and this seemed an opportunity I shouldn't miss, so I accepted the invitation for six days in Harare from the 30th of September to the 5th of October. The Foundation paid for hotel accommodation and economy airfares. I didn't relish making such a long return journey in economy, but Secker and Penguin generously upgraded me to business class. I decided to add a few extra days at my own expense in order to see a bit more of the country, and arranged with a Harare travel agent a three-day package tour by air to Victoria Falls and the Hwange National Safari Park.

It was an exciting prospect, but when I began to prepare for the whole trip I was unsettled by health warnings from various sources about the dangers of contracting malaria where I was headed. One leaflet began ominously, 'No antimalarial drugs are 100% effective', and it seemed that of the two principal preventative medicines, the more effective one could cause psychosis. I never quite cast off the apprehension that sub-Saharan Africa was a dangerous place for visitors from northern Europe, and it did not give me confidence that on my very first day, strolling in downtown Harare, I barked my shin forcibly on a low concrete bollard which had escaped my notice, placed in the middle of a broad pedestrian sidewalk for no discernible purpose. The pain gave me a restless night, and next day the leg had swelled up around an ugly haematoma, requiring treatment later in the week.

During that week various events – meals, readings and excursions – were arranged for the visiting writers by the team managing the Awards, who were mostly academics from the University of Zimbabwe in Harare, the country's leading institution of higher education, and the cultural administrators in the government. Some of them were also judging our work in small groups at the same time, and we writers found it slightly awkward to be making conversation with people who over the same period were discussing our work and deciding its fate. We had seen lists of the books in contention in advance and I had read a few of those nominated for the Best Novel award before leaving home. I was impressed by an epic novel with elements of magic realism set in nineteenth-century India and modern America called *Red Earth and Pouring Rain*, by Vikram Chandra, who when I met him turned out to be a charming young man, bubbling over with delight at being part of the event. I had also read Rohinton Mistry's *A Fine Balance*, which I thought was likely to win the prize. It is a long novel describing in evocative detail the lives of four young Indian men from varied backgrounds who come to live together in a city at a time of political tension in the country. I was sure it would win the prize not only because it was a masterpiece of realistic fiction, but also because it was so appropriate for a 'Commonwealth' award. *Therapy* had no Commonwealth associations at all, and furthermore another British novel, Louis de Bernières' *Captain Corelli's Mandolin*, had won the prize in the previous year, so the judges would be disposed to avoid a repetition. Mistry had emigrated from India to Canada in 1973, taking Canadian nationality soon afterwards, and so qualified for nomination in the 'region' of Canada and the Caribbean.

Our hosts made sure we were fully occupied during the week. On one day I had a radio interview, a visit to a shopping mall, a book signing in a bookshop, a visit to an art gallery, and a meeting with Zimbabwean writers in the Methodist Church hall, followed by a drinks reception at the University hosted by the Vice Chancellor and his wife. I was fortunate in having an introduction to someone in Harare who had nothing to do with the Commonwealth Prize – Tim McLoughlin, who taught English Language and Literature at the University. It originated from Jim Boulton, who was Head of the Department of English at Birmingham University. Jim had joined the RAF in 1943 after completing his first year as an undergraduate

85

at Durham University and trained to fly Spitfires in Rhodesia. He was about to take part in an attack on occupied Singapore in 1945 when, fortunately for him, Japan surrendered and he was able to return safely to Durham and begin a distinguished scholarly career. But he had fond memories of Rhodesia, and established an academic link with the University in Harare, bringing some of its brightest students to Birmingham for postgraduate study, which was how he got to know and like the McLoughlins. Tim and his wife Dorothy were Irish Catholics. They were a salt-of-the-earth couple who did much charitable work – for example, helping single mothers of children born with HIV – and I took to them at once.

This was a time when President Mugabe, once regarded as an enlightened Head of State, was showing signs of the ruthless dictator he later became. Tim was depressed by the policy known as 'indigenisation' or 'Africanisation' which Mugabe was imposing on the University's appointment of staff, because it was lowering the standards of teaching and research and creating an inefficient and obstructive administrative bureaucracy. I sympathised, but one institution I had observed in Harare seemed to be immune from this policy. One day the visiting writers were taken to see a boys' boarding school which meticulously imitated British prep schools and public schools almost to the point of parody, the pupils wearing a uniform of blazers, ties and grey flannel trousers or shorts, and displaying impeccable manners to the visitors. The teachers were mostly British, and the pupils were the sons of affluent Zimbabweans who evidently thought this style of education appropriate to their status. It seemed that the trappings of the old Empire still retained prestige at a certain level of society.

The climax of the whole week was a gala dinner and prize-giving ceremony at Harare's poshest hotel, attended by all the writers and officials involved in the competition. One of the guests was Doris Lessing and I was delighted to be seated next to her. We had met once before, and she remembered the occasion, though at this distance in time I cannot. I was a great admirer of her novel *The Golden Notebook*, which was one of the seminal books of the sixties on account of its radical feminist perspective and formal experimentation, and I had written about it in the title essay of *The Novelist at the Crossroads*. Lessing combined realistic fictional narration with visionary and surrealistic writing in subsequent novels, most impressively I thought in *Briefing for a Descent into Hell*, which I reviewed enthusiastically in the *New Statesman*. She had emigrated to England in 1949, but still felt an attachment to the country she knew as Rhodesia in her childhood and young adulthood, and wrote movingly about its racial tensions in her first novel, *The Grass is Singing*. She frequently returned to Zimbabwe with a mission to encourage reading and writing there, especially among children and young people, and she organised regular consignments of books from England to be distributed to schools and libraries. A lending library in rural areas, she told me, was often a cardboard box under a tree. She impressed me as completely unaffected by her literary fame, and her first reaction, according to one report, on hearing that she had won the Nobel Prize in 2007 – '*Bloody hell!*' – was entirely in character.

Our conversation was terminated prematurely because of a procedural mix-up. After the first course had been served, Dr Malabar, a senior member of the University and chief administrator of the Prize, came to our table to say that a government minister had failed to arrive as guest of honour at the top table, and would Doris please replace him. She was reluctant, but submitted graciously. I heard later that Malabar had wanted to make the Vice Chancellor of the University the guest of honour, and had initially resisted the suggestions of his colleagues that Doris Lessing would be a more appropriate choice, as indeed she deserved to be. Later in the evening he made a long and fulsome speech in praise of the VC which provoked a wag at the back of the room to call out, 'All right! All right! You've got the job!' Malabar was unfazed and continued his speech to the end. I had to admire his cool. He had helped me to arrange my brief tour, which formed a link between us, and had told me confidentially the day before that *A Fine Balance* had won the Prize against *Therapy* by a narrow margin, and that I could consider myself the runner-up, though later the Australian novelist Gillian Mears was officially paired with me in that category for her novel *The Grass Sister*.

The award of the main prize was something of an anti-climax, because Rohinton Mistry was not present to accept it. No explanation was given for his absence, officially or unofficially. It was however reported a few months later that he had an audience with the Queen at Buckingham Palace, so there must have been a good reason for his non-appearance in Harare. I was delighted that Vikram Chandra won the prize for Best First Novel. The rest of us who were present as winners in the various regions stepped up to receive our consolation cheques from the hand of Doris Lessing, and the event was over.

Next day the writers dispersed to catch their flights and I embarked on my brief sightseeing tour. I spent an enjoyable day viewing the famous Victoria Falls, which were not as spectacular as they usually are because it was the dry season and the volume of the cascades was diminished, but it was still a sublime panorama to behold. I watched, queasily, as gung-ho young people bungee-jumped from a crag hundreds of feet above the lake. Only a loaded gun held to my head could persuade me to do the same. My guide was a pleasant but melancholic young man whose name was Deo Gratias, like the loyal servant of Graham Greene's hero in *A Burnt Out Case*, a coincidence that delighted me. He was Catholic of course, twenty-seven years old, married with a young baby, and spoke wistfully of wanting to go to England to find a better job.

In the afternoon I was taken on a Sundowner cruise on the Zambesi River – '*Enjoy sipping a cool drink and watch the animals come down to the water's edge,'* my brochure urged, and I did just that, well covered against the mosquitoes, but few animals made an appearance. I decided to postpone the operation on my leg and observe some from the veranda of my hotel room, where breakfast was delivered each morning. It faced east and the rising sun cast a wonderful light on the animals who gathered at a waterhole not far away. Next morning the veranda was invaded by a group of small monkeys who tried to steal scones and fruit from my table. I had to go to the bathroom and when I came back into my bed-sitting room, having carelessly left the veranda door ajar, I found the monkeys swarming all over it, climbing on to the shelves and swinging from the central light fixture. I managed to shoo them out by shouting and waving my arms, but one very small monkey climbed up to the top of the mosquito curtains and refused to come down, so I had to phone reception for a porter who came and removed him.

Next day I flew to Hwange, Zimbabwe's largest National Park, to stay at a safari lodge on the edge of it. I was met at the airport along with another passenger, a big blonde woman who was going to the same place, and had with her two huge cases so heavy the meeter and greeter could hardly lift them. She explained that they contained photographic equipment, and told me that she wrote books about the environment in various parts of the world illustrated with her own photographs. Sandra was an adventurous lady, and over lunch beside the hotel pool she told me about some of her experiences in other African safari parks. She was once with a group of tourists who had left their jeeps and were being led on foot by their guide through the bush in what he assured them was a safe area, when unexpectedly an angry elephant was reported to be approaching. The guide told the tourists to scatter and hide themselves behind tree trunks. But since several were elderly and deaf this announcement caused considerable confusion and panic – which as someone prone to anxiety and partially deaf myself, I could easily imagine.

I made a resolution not to dismount from the 'safari drive' we were due to take in the park that evening, which of course turned out to be perfectly safe. We joined a procession of twelve jeeps occupied by tourists from other lodges and hotels. This number of vehicles detracted somewhat from a feeling of privileged access to nature in the wild, but the vehicles separated once we were inside the park, and we saw zebras, giraffes, ostriches, buffaloes and warthogs from our solitary jeep. Elephants too. Hwange Park is one of the last elephant sanctuaries in Africa, and observing these magnificent creatures at close range in their natural habitat was the high point of the excursion for me.

I returned to Harare and prepared for my flight home in the evening of the next day, much of which I spent with the McLoughlins. Knowing that I had time to kill they invited me to spend it with them, and I was very grateful. I was now feeling extremely tired because I had fitted so much activity into little more than a week, and was longing to get home. I took a taxi to arrive early at the airport. Inside the small airport building I spent my remaining Zimbabwe currency on a necklace made of multi-coloured glass for Mary, and sat with a book for a couple of hours on a moulded upright chair in a Departure Lounge which hardly deserved that designation, though I'm sure the airport is much grander today. I had travelled out via Frankfurt by Lufthansa, but my return journey was a direct flight by British Airways to Heathrow, which was just what I desired. I slept well.

9

1995 was an exceptionally busy and eventful year for me. In April I received an invitation to take part in the Chicago Humanities Festival, an annual event which took place over a weekend early in November. Each Festival had a theme, such as 'Crime and Punishment' and 'Communication and Understanding'. This year it was 'Love and Marriage'. I was invited to give a speech (as it was called, rather than a lecture) on 'Love and Marriage in Fiction'. This theme was right up my street, and connected opportunely with the recent publication of *Therapy* in America. The description given of other events in the Festival was also enticing, so I wrote to accept. Any doubts I might have had were settled by a fax from the Chief Executive of the Festival, Eileen Mackevich, confirming and welcoming my acceptance, which concluded: 'We are pleased to provide you with an honorarium of $3000, as well as first class round trip flight from Birmingham to Chicago on American Airlines.' Three thousand dollars for one speech and a few days' social participation in the Festival! I could hardly believe it. I learned later that the Festival was produced by the Illinois Humanities Council with the help of wealthy individual and corporate sponsors who liked to be associated with its high-minded cultural mission; but even so, I was astonished by the lavish expenditure attached to my visit.

Earlier that same year I had received an invitation to visit the Iowa Writers' Workshop, a postgraduate programme in creative writing at the University of Iowa's Champaign-Urbana campus. It was the mother of all creative writing degree courses, Iowa being the first University to establish such a programme in the USA, and probably the world, in 1936. Over the following decades its status and prestige continued to increase and at the time of my invitation it was generally regarded as the best of its kind, receiving a deluge of applications every year. Students who were admitted were likely to be contacted almost immediately by New York literary agents offering their services. Probably my invitation was initiated when somebody on the staff noticed that I would be speaking at the Humanities Festival in Chicago, from where Champaign-Urbana is a short flight. I was curious to see what this legendary institution was like, and arranged to visit for a few days before the Festival began. I was asked to give a reading to the Workshop's staff and students in the evening of the day after my arrival, to do a Q&A session with the students on the second day, and otherwise chat informally with anyone who was interested in meeting me.

I had never flown first class before, and the prospect of experiencing it *gratis* was one of the attractions of the trip for me. I was aware that the full luxury of this form of travel could only be experienced on the huge Boeing 747 which had space for all kinds of amenities like bars and complimentary manicures. American Airlines flew a smaller-sized three-engine jet on the Birmingham–Chicago route, but they tried to compensate for the limitation of space with their First Class meal service, enticingly described in a twelve-page brochure elegantly printed on imitation vellum, which was handed to First Class passengers after boarding. The menu was a rhetorical *tour de force* which I kept as a souvenir. This begins with 'An assortment of warm Roasted Nuts to accompany your preferred Cocktail or Beverage'. It was the adjective 'warm' which to me most poignantly expressed the menu writer's determination to make the meal seem truly First Class. Not cold, hard, brittle nuts – perish the thought – but nuts carefully warmed just enough to bring out the flavour and soften the bite of each kernel. The lavish five-course luncheon was deliciously decadent, with only the finest caviar on offer, and there was an Afternoon Meal with several options for passengers who felt peckish later. At the back of the brochure there were several pages of information about the videos available and how to view them in your seat. But like most of the replete passengers I reclined mine and slept for much of the afternoon.

I flew to Chicago O'Hare and then on to Cedar Rapids, the airport that serves Iowa City where the Writers' Workshop is situated, and was met by an Asian Indian student who drove me to the University's hotel, and took me to an Indian restaurant for supper. He had a Master's degree from the Workshop and was now doing a PhD on translation. Next morning, which was bright and crisp, I set off to find the Workshop. Students, singly and in groups, all wearing blue jeans and carrying their books in rucksacks, showed me the way. I noticed the Prairie Lights Bookshop, presumably named in imitation of, or homage to, the City Lights shop in San Francisco famously associated with the Beat Poets, and went inside. I introduced myself to the manager and signed some copies of my novels for the shop. Spotting a book on display called *Midair* by Frank Conroy, the Director of the Writers' Workshop, I tried to buy it, but the manager insisted on giving it to me.

Frank Conroy had been in his position since 1987 and would continue in it till 2005. I had first encountered his name in 1969 when writing the title essay of *The Novelist at the Crossroads*. His debut book, *Stop-Time*, an autobiography published in 1967 when he was only thirty-one, was a big success, praised by Norman Mailer for having 'the intimate and unprotected candour of a novel'. I cited it in my essay as an example of the 'non-fiction novel' which was one of the stylistic options available to contemporary writers. *Midair* was a volume of short stories, published eighteen years later, and it would be another eight years before Conroy's next novel, *Body and Soul*, appeared. Teaching creative writing full time inevitably takes its toll on the teacher's own creativity, which is why I engaged in it only for short periods at long intervals. The more conscientious the teacher is about reading and commenting on the students' work – and they were obviously *very* conscientious in the Iowa Writers' Workshop – the more likely it is to become a drain on their own imaginative energy, and perhaps to make them compulsive revisers, slow to finish work in progress and reluctant to expose it to judgement. I was told that Frank Conroy had destroyed the manuscripts of at least two novels. He was a big man, youthful looking for his age, casually dressed like everybody in the Workshop. He greeted me warmly and we chatted in his office before he took me to lunch. He said he had just returned from a three-day engagement in Germany, and when I expressed surprise at so brief a long-haul trip, he said he always travelled first class. I nodded sagely as if to imply, 'Of course'. He enquired about two British novelists he knew, Ian McEwan and Graham Swift, and asked me about the movement to abolish the Net Book Agreement in the UK.[1] He said the conditions for

---

[1] This required bookshops to sell new books at the price set by the publishers, but in the eighties and nineties many publishers, including my own, were eager to abolish it in order to boost sales by selective discounting. Increasingly the NBA was flouted and eventually it was judged to be illegal. Subsequently few books were sold for the price on the cover. Most people in publishing now regard the effects of this change as disastrous, especially for authors and independent booksellers.

publishing literary fiction in the USA were very bad and I commiserated, although I had never known them to be described in any other way. Somebody told me later he had got half a million dollars for the movie rights of *Body and Soul*, but disappointing reviews for the book.

My first event was the 'reading' that evening to an audience of staff and students. Frank Conroy told me I would be introduced by Marilynne Robinson, who I gathered was the star of the teaching staff, and regarded with some awe by the students. I was aware of her first novel, *Housekeeping*, though I hadn't read it. It was published in the US in 1980, and was a finalist for the Pulitzer Prize and well received when it was published in England shortly afterwards, but she had published nothing since. In fact, it wasn't until 2004 that she published her second novel, *Gilead*, which was highly praised on both sides of the Atlantic and given several awards, from which time her reputation continued to grow. The long introduction to the Wikipedia article about her concludes: 'In November 2015 the *New York Review of Books* published a two-part conversation between Marilynne Robinson and President Obama, covering topics in American history and the role of faith in society.' An American writer could hardly rise higher in the cultural pecking order than that.

Such fame for Marilynne Robinson was hidden in the mists of the future when I took my seat in the front row of the small auditorium that served the Writers' Workshop for events of this kind, and waited for her to introduce me from the stage, after which I was to step up and do my piece. I had met her briefly at a drinks reception beforehand, and she had seemed rather aloof and uncommunicative. She came on to the stage from the wings and began to speak, without a microphone. If I hadn't been sitting in the front row, I would not have heard her because of my impaired hearing. After a politely complimentary summary of my career she shifted into a personal, anecdotal mode, and suddenly I was paying close attention. She said she had been a graduate student at Brown University in 1963, taking a creative writing course under the novelist Jack John Hawkes, and that I had been a member of the class. The students took turns to read from their work to the group, and she recalled an occasion when I read from something of mine which was intended to be comic but failed to have its intended effect. 'I wanted to laugh,' she said, 'but I couldn't because nobody else was laughing.' She went on to say that happily I had put that early failure behind me and 'Now we have all learned to laugh at David Lodge's writing.'

I listened to this story with growing astonishment. I first set foot on American soil in August 1964, not 1963, on a year's unpaid leave from Birmingham University, as the recipient of a Harkness Fellowship for study and travel in the USA. I spent the fall semester of that year at Brown University reading American Literature and sitting in on a graduate seminar run by Mark Spilka on modern American fiction. To my regret, John Hawkes was on sabbatical leave from Brown in the academic year 1964–5, and our paths crossed only once, when we met during one weekend at the University of Virginia in the spring of 1965. Marilynne Robinson's reminiscence, I thought, must be a case of mistaken identity, confusing me with some British graduate student who was in John Hawkes' class in 1963, but it put me in a potentially embarrassing position. How was I to respond to her introduction when I stepped up on to the stage? To thank her for it without any qualification went against the grain, but to reveal that her anecdote could not possibly be true would humiliate her in the presence of her colleagues and students. On the spur of the moment I began my talk by saying lightly, 'Well, I've never been introduced with a short story before,' which caused a ripple of amusement in the audience, and then carried on with my *Therapy* reading. I was hoping to talk to Marilynne after the event and quietly set the record straight, but I did not see her again that evening, or the next day when I was back in the Workshop for the Q&A session, and the day after that I returned to Chicago. Marilynne may have picked up the implication in my remark that her anecdote was a fiction and perhaps begun to doubt the reliability of her own memory, but couldn't bring herself to check it out with me. When I returned home I wrote a letter to her explaining why I could not possibly have been in John Hawkes' class at the same time as her, but she did not reply.

Apart from that unresolved enigma, my brief visit to the Writers' Workshop passed agreeably. The Question and Answer session with the students went well, and a member of the admin staff wrote in a letter afterwards that 'Frank Conroy couldn't stop talking about it'. I also took opportunities to chat more casually to the students, but it was difficult to draw them out about their own work. It seemed strange in some ways that these talented and ambitious young people had been gathered together in a quiet provincial town on the flat mid-western plain, far from cities like New York, Chicago and San Francisco, where new writing was constantly being produced, reviewed, circulated, and discussed, interacting only with their teachers and each other. A Jewish student called Nathan told me that coming to Iowa City was the biggest culture shock he had ever experienced: 'The peace and quiet, the innocence, the low cost of living . . .' But this environment had been deliberately chosen to nourish creativity and aid concentration. The Writers' Workshop was like a monastic institution: its religion literature, with the teachers as monks, the students as novices, and the salvation to which all aspired being successful publication.

I flew to Chicago the next day and checked in at the Ritz-Carlton hotel where a bedroom and sitting room had been reserved for me over the weekend of the Festival. I had been invited to dine that evening with Father Andrew Greeley, a remarkable man whom I would be meeting for the first time, though we had corresponded for several years. He was a Catholic priest, but at the same time a professor of Sociology at the University of Chicago, a journalist who contributed articles to major American newspapers, wrote a weekly column in the *Chicago Sun-Times*, and was a bestselling novelist. Our relationship began when he sent me one of his novels, having read some of my own and perceived that I was a liberal Catholic like himself, especially on the issue of birth control. Andrew bravely challenged the teaching of *Humanae Vitae*, and used his sociological skills to conduct a survey which showed that most Catholic married couples in America ignored it. He was a thorn in the flesh of the conservative clerical hierarchy, especially Cardinal Cody of his own Chicago diocese, and was one of the first American writers to expose evidence of sexual abuse by Catholic clergy and the hierarchy's concealment of it.

He went on sending me his novels, sometimes two at once, and they became something of an embarrassment for several reasons. They were not what I would call literary novels, but middle-brow fiction, usually with a Catholic story. I skimmed through some, but did not have time to read them properly, or room on my bookshelves to store them. But I always acknowledged receipt of them, expressing a genuine admiration for his productivity, which was quite extraordinary. He published seventy novels in his lifetime and about as many non-fiction books on a wide range of subjects, the first of which was entitled *The Social Effects of Catholic Education* (1961) and the last was *A Stupid, Unjust and Criminal War: Iraq 2001–2007*, published in the latter year. Some of his novels, like *Cardinal Sins*, sold millions of copies and made him a rich man, but he gave generously from his earnings to charities and deserving causes. The most surprising feature of his novels was that they often contained explicit descriptions of sex between married couples, written with gusto. Andrew believed that sexual pleasure was a gift from God, citing the *Song of Songs* in support, and celebrated it accordingly. Many of his coreligionists were scandalised and said so, but he was unperturbed. When people asked him how a priest could write knowledgeably about sex he attributed it to his experience as a confessor. It seems likely that writing these novels was for him a kind of imaginative release from the constraints of celibacy. Asked why he published so many he replied, 'I suppose I have an Irish weakness for words gone wild. Besides, if you're celibate, you must do something.'

Andrew Greeley was well aware that there had been a steep decline in the number of vocations for the priesthood in America, as in Europe, and that in an era when sexuality was openly discussed, depicted, and recognised as fundamental to human nature, young Catholic men, however strong their faith, were reluctant to commit themselves to lifetime celibacy. He proposed a solution, based on the assumption that there were devout and idealistic young Catholic men who would be prepared to dedicate ten years to serving the community as priests if they could then return with honour to the lay state, free to find a wife and produce a family. This seemed to me an imaginative proposal, a holy equivalent to Voluntary Service Overseas, but the Vatican and the American Catholic hierarchy showed no interest in the idea.

Andrew, who like me was in his sixties at this time, but looking in good trim, with an upright posture, neatly dressed in a well-fitting black suit with clerical collar, entertained me to dinner that evening at a restaurant in the John Hancock Center, where he occupied an apartment. It is an elegant modernist skyscraper, one hundred floors high, and an icon of Chicago, which contains some of the finest modern architecture in the world. In the corridors of O'Hare airport I saw posters urging travellers to fly to Birmingham by American Airlines, but wisely they did not feature a picture of Brum's city centre to invite comparison. After dinner Andrew led me to an observation point near the top of the John Hancock Center, which gave an amazing panoramic view of the city spread out in glittering rectangles of light, the typical grid system of American roads illuminated by street lighting and moving traffic stretching, it seemed, to the horizon.

Then he took me to his apartment. It was as spacious as I expected and meticulously furnished in a style that expressed its occupant. The large living room was a kind of study, with top of the range computers, printers, conference telephone and other gadgetry laid out on desks and tables of dark polished wood, and a huge TV in one corner. But the room was also a kind of shrine, with framed photographs of Andrew alone and with groups hung on the walls, and objects arranged on shelves which were awards or gifts from identified admirers and institutions. Everything was orderly, immaculately clean and polished, the work of a housekeeper who came in every day. I congratulated him on his splendid apartment and thanked him for his hospitality. He escorted me to the elevator and we shook hands. I had little doubt that he would return immediately to his desk and spend some hours writing before he went to bed. I did not meet him in person again.[2]

The Festival officially began the next morning, with a guided tour for guest participants of the Monet exhibition currently showing at the Art Institute of Chicago. It was billed as the biggest ever retrospective of the artist's work, the Institute's own permanent collection of Monets having been enlarged by loans from galleries and private owners around the world. The Monets were indeed

---

[2] The end of Andrew Greeley's life was tragic. He died in hospital in 2013, five years after a freak accident, when part of his overcoat was trapped in the door of a cab as he left it. The driver drove off without noticing his plight and he was dragged along the road for some distance, sustaining injuries to his brain which ended his career. After a long hospitalisation he lived in his Chicago home as a chronic invalid, the object of pity and dismay to his many friends and admirers. How, one wonders, could he reconcile this horrible fate with his faith in the God he had served so diligently according to his lights? I cannot imagine that it would be possible.

wonderful, but the painting in the Institute that most impressed me was Georges Seurat's 'A Sunday Afternoon on the Island of La Grande Jatte', that famous picture, which I had known hitherto only in reproductions, of Parisian folk standing, sitting or reclining on a grassy bank of the Seine in high summer, mostly depicted in profile gazing at the river, perfectly still, as if enchanted, or dazed by the heat. Stephen Sondheim wrote a wonderful musical inspired by this painting, called *Sunday in the Park with George*, which Mary and I saw later at the National Theatre in London. The first act ended unforgettably with a tableau of the cast dressed and posed exactly as in the painting. Nothing in the second act could match it.

My main contribution to the Festival, the speech on 'Love and Marriage in Fiction', was scheduled to begin at 6 p.m. at the St James Episcopal Cathedral, and I delivered my talk from the pulpit, high above the pews. I began by saying: 'The missing link in this festival's official title, one might say, is sex. I belong to the last British generation for whom marriage was the only socially approved way of having sex, and I was brought up in the Roman Catholic Church, in which marriage is the only morally approved way of having sex. There was a special twist to the Catholic teaching on this matter, in that when you finally succeeded in getting married you had to choose between having less sex than you wanted or more babies than you wanted.' There is a large Catholic population in Chicago, and the laughter that rose up from the congregation suggested that a number of them were Catholics and some had probably read *The British Museum Is Falling Down* and *How Far Can You Go?*

Although love and marriage are elements in some of the earliest narrative literature that has survived, such as the Homeric epics, those stories were originally told in the form of oral poetry. I said that it was prose fiction, the realistic novel of contemporary life which evolved in Europe in the eighteenth century and became the culturally dominant form of literature in the next two centuries, which made the relationship between love and marriage its favourite subject, exploring conflict as well as complementarity between these two human experiences, in the works of great novelists like Jane Austen, George Eliot, Thomas Hardy, Henry James, D.H. Lawrence and their successors. I concluded with some observations about the effects on contemporary fiction of sexual liberation, second-wave feminism, and the abolition of censorship. The audience seemed to enjoy this helter-skelter survey, and Eileen Mackevich and her colleagues were delighted.

That day and the next I met several other British guest speakers, some of whom, like Michael Holroyd and Margaret Drabble I knew well, and others, such as Marina Warner, I met for the first time and thus began a new friendship. Most of us I think were amazed by the lavish scale of the Festival, and the imaginative mixture of events it comprised. There were forty-five in all, ranging from 'Love and Marriage in Pharaonic Egypt' to 'Lesbians at Home: Love and Power in Gay Relationships', all squeezed into two days, so it was not possible to attend more than a few. I didn't go to Andrew Greeley's lecture on 'Love and Marriage: the Catholic Perspective', because he had already given me a copy of the text, but I did enjoy 'A Sunday Conversation with Stephen Sondheim', who was seated at a piano to add musical illustrations to his discourse. The highlight of the Festival for me was a dramatisation of 'The Divorce Trial of Henry VIII' performed in the auditorium of the Field Natural History Museum. It was imaginatively staged with the Monarch and his Queen, Katherine of Aragon, dressed in Elizabethan costume, while the lawyers who debated the rights and wrongs of Henry's divorce suit were played by Chicago lawyers wearing modern suits. The audience acted as jury and the verdict predictably went against Henry. Afterwards there was a fundraising Benefit Dinner served enterprisingly in the main exhibition hall of the museum on round tables with white napery and gleaming cutlery, laid out between and beneath the stuffed wild animals of different continents and periods. The evening epitomised the Festival for me as a life-enhancing collaboration between high culture and big money.

On the 13th of November, the day I returned from Chicago to Birmingham, my friend Ian Gregor died, and a week later I attended his funeral in Canterbury, where he had lived for many years. He was one of my oldest friends, whose company I always enjoyed. I kept in regular contact with him, yet I have said very little about him in my memoirs, apart from mentioning in *QAGTTBB* that he obtained the very first university job I applied for before I knew him personally, and that I got to know him later through mutual friends in Birmingham, and as one of a circle of Catholic academic literary critics who met occasionally at Spode Priory to discuss matters of common interest. This seems an appropriate place to say more. He belonged to a staunch Catholic family in Newcastle, and obtained his first degree at the city's University. He was called up for National Service and opted to do his time in the local coal mines – an alternative that was offered to young men in the region in those days of coal shortages. He told me once, over a nightcap of single malt, what a shock his initiation was: his first job, deep underground, was assisting a man who despatched coal in trucks drawn on rails by a female donkey. He was devoted to this animal and, as he made clear to Ian, used her for sexual relief. Nobody who knew Ian only in adult life would have guessed that he had been exposed to such experience in youth. After his release from the mines and graduation from Newcastle he studied at Oxford, taught at Edinburgh University, and eventually moved, with his friend Mark Kinkead-Weekes, to the new University of Kent in Canterbury where he stayed for the rest of his life.

He was something of a chameleon in character. From the little I observed of him as a teacher and administrator he was rather formal and even severe in those roles, but in private with his friends he was full of fun and wit. At an Eng. Lit. conference a group of us were sitting together drinking beer. When someone mentioned Coleridge's poem 'The Rime of the Ancient Mariner', he cut in with: 'Ah yes! The Ancient Mariner, a terrible goalkeeper ... He stoppeth one in three.' Typically, he laughed at the jest as heartily as the rest of us. There was something of the performer about Ian, a relishing of the words he uttered. He was a bachelor of a now rare kind, apparently quite content with a celibate single life but sociable and gregarious. He enjoyed good food and drink, and playing golf with his friends, loved parties, and hosted a large one to celebrate the Kent strawberry season every summer. He had several women friends but no intimate relationship with any of them as far as I was aware, and he certainly wasn't gay.

As a scholar and critic he was particularly interested in William Golding and Thomas Hardy, and published a book about the latter's novels called *The Great Web* in 1974. One summer, when he was writing that book, I accepted an invitation to join him in a short tour of Dorset, the main inspiration for a fictional territory in south-west England that Hardy called 'Wessex'. It was a very pleasant few days, beginning at the museum in Dorchester ('Casterbridge' in the novels) where there is a replica of Hardy's study behind glass. I was told on good authority that once a scholar was permitted to sit at the desk, which was Hardy's own, and make notes about the books and papers on its surface, and that some tourists visiting the museum were heard to say, nudging each other, 'Look – there's Thomas Hardy!'

Ian drove us around the gorgeous Dorset countryside, pausing at places associated with Hardy and his novels. When we stayed in small inns and B&Bs, Ian always asked for a twin-bed room to save the expense of separate accommodation, and I occasionally glimpsed a speculative or disapproving look in the eyes of a receptionist which made me feel a little uncomfortable, but I am sure it never crossed Ian's mind that anyone could suppose we were a couple.

Once when reminiscing to me about the Salesian grammar

school he attended in Newcastle, he recalled the bolder boys in the sixth form teasing the old priest who took them for religious instruction by asking casuistical questions, like 'How far can you go with a girl, Father, before it's a sin?' The story stuck in my mind and gave me the title for the novel I was working on at the time, and in gratitude I dedicated *How Far Can You Go?* to Ian. After I presented a copy to him I had misgivings about how he would respond to its candid sexual content. I asked him later if he had been shocked by it and he admitted that it had been somewhat disconcerting to 'a single Catholic gentleman like myself'. The old-fashioned formality of 'gentleman' was a typical rhetorical touch.

In late middle age Ian began to have health problems. Once when he was staying with Mary and me in Birmingham he received an urgent message from his doctor who had just received the result of a test which revealed some condition requiring immediate treatment, and he had to rush back to Canterbury. Later concern was aroused by a bump on his balding pate which seemed to be growing alarmingly. A benign cyst was diagnosed and an operation performed to remove it. Unfortunately, something went wrong with the procedure and Ian had a stroke while under anaesthetic which badly affected one side of his body and handicapped him for the rest of his life. He continued to live in the modern townhouse he owned near the County cricket ground on the outskirts of Canterbury, though with two flights of stairs it was unsuitable, and eventually he had a bad fall which effectively confined him to the house. He was helped by a loyal band of friends, male and female, who did his shopping and kept him company. But for the man who loved golf and pubs and parties and driving through the countryside the last years of his life must have been almost unbearable, though he bore them bravely without any trace of self-pity. I continued to visit him and one evening I ventured to ask if his faith had made it easier for him to accept his misfortune. He pondered the question silently for what seemed a long time, and then very slowly shook his head. I admired and respected his honesty. I thought that Andrew Greeley would probably have given the same answer.

I regretted that Mary had not been able to accompany me to Chicago, as she would certainly have enjoyed the experience. But since our last trip together to America in 1981 she had developed an aversion to air travel, especially long haul, and could only tolerate flights of not more than three or four hours' duration. She was enjoying life at home now that she had retired from her position as a teacher of 18+ students with Special Needs at Handsworth Technical College. She had served that department very well, and was probably the most highly qualified member of the staff, but being part time she had never had the status and salary that she deserved. Now she was free to indulge her own interests, one of which was art. She enrolled in a painting class at our local Further Education centre, and enjoyed it so much that she decided to do a degree in Fine Art.

There were artistic genes in Mary's family. Her father's sister, 'Aunt Alice', was a respected watercolour painter in Ireland, one of whose works had passed into Mary's hands and hung on a wall in our house. Her own elder sister, Eileen, taught art in secondary schools in England and later Canada, and in her eighties still sells her own watercolour landscapes without difficulty. Watercolour is not much favoured as a medium by today's art colleges, and Bournville College of Art was no exception, but that was fine by Mary who was open to experiment and variety in art. She registered as a part-time student at Bournville, which was a suburban branch of the Birmingham School of Art in the centre of the city. It specialised in teaching a one-year foundation course preparatory to the full degree course, and occupied a cluster of buildings around Bournville Village Green. The foundation course was just what Mary wanted, requiring students to try their hands at all kinds of visual and three-dimensional art in different media, and she produced some amazing work in that year, notably a sundial for our rear garden. It has a tilted pyramidal base, cast in concrete by Mary herself, surmounted by a horizontal brass plate with a dial of the hours engraved to her own design by a workshop in the Birmingham Jewellery Quarter. She learned to use acrylic paint on canvas, and to use computers and cameras as tools for art. Her main presentation at the end of the BA course consisted of colour images obtained from photographing the surface and banks of a local canal and then hugely magnifying details in them so that they resembled abstract paintings or imaginary landscapes. Another of her projects, which I gladly subsidised, was a slide show projected on to the walls of Bournville's carillon tower to the accompaniment of the bells. It was advertised and attracted a good crowd of spectators one summer evening.

She acquired a new circle of friends at the College, mature women like herself who desired to express themselves through art. Several of them were working class rather than middle class and had needed considerable determination to achieve this ambition in spite of family opposition. Mary's commitment to art was good for our marriage as well as for herself, because it was an interest I could share – not as a practitioner, though I once joined her for a week's course in life drawing and painting at West Dean, a College in Sussex which offers short residential courses for beginners and improvers – but as an appreciative viewer of her own work and of fine art generally. Since I acquired the flat in London we had gone to many more exhibitions great and small, and extended our knowledge of modern art and art history together.

Both of us admired the work of Paula Rego, a Portuguese painter who had studied at the Slade School of Fine Art in University College London at about the same time that Mary and I were students in the English Department there, though we were not then aware of her existence. She settled in England after graduating from the Slade, while continuing to draw inspiration from her native country and its culture. By lucky chance we eventually got to know her personally. In 2001 Paula was commissioned to do a series of lithographs to illustrate an edition of Charlotte Brontë's classic novel *Jane Eyre* for Thames & Hudson. My former publisher at Secker & Warburg, Tom Rosenthal, knew her well and had produced superbly illustrated books about her art. He also sat for a striking portrait of himself by her which hung in the living room of his house in Primrose Hill. Tom wrote to me to say that Paula wanted to read some feminist literary criticism about *Jane Eyre* in preparation for her project, and asked if I could suggest some sources. I was glad to do so, and attached a copy of my own essay, 'Fire and Eyre: Charlotte Brontë's War of Earthly Elements'. Although it was first published in my book *Language of Fiction* in 1966, well before the new wave of feminist criticism which started with Germaine Greer's *The Female Eunuch* in 1991, its gist was compatible with the spirit of that movement.

One day I was sent the brochure for a charity auction of pictures in various media generously donated by established artists. One of these works was a large lithograph by Paula Rego in black on white called 'Jane Eyre', one of the illustrations she had created for the Thames & Hudson book. Daringly it depicted the heroine of the novel from behind, covered from shoulders to ankles in a black, full-skirted Victorian dress, and apparently walking towards the entrance to a totally black and inscrutable space beyond. The effect was not forbidding, for there was a strength in the purposeful figure which expressed her determination to resist the dark, negative elements in her life. It was a fascinating picture, and I wanted to possess it, so I went to the auction. It was the first time I had bid for anything at such an event. When 'Jane Eyre' was presented and the bidding began it soon became clear that I had one determined competitor for the picture, a lady in another part of the audience whom I couldn't see but who evidently wanted it as keenly as I did, which is just what an auctioneer desires. Other bidders quickly dropped out as the price rose higher and higher, until it approached £2500. When I bid that figure, there was a pause. The auctioneer looked enquiringly towards the lady, who must have shaken her head, so the picture was knocked down to me, to general applause. It was probably above the market price at the time, but I never regretted my purchase, which now hangs in our sitting room in Edgbaston.

Paula and her friend, companion, and occasional model, the writer Anthony Rudolf, were pleased when they heard of my purchase of the lithograph, and contacted me. Soon we were invited to Paula's studio which was a fascinating experience. Paula, who was then in her sixties, was a vortex of energy moving around the studio, working on several paintings in progress. I noticed a small, unframed but striking pastel portrait of a seated teenage girl, which was on the floor, propped up against the skirting board, and I remarked on it to Paula. 'Oh, I'm throwing that away,' she said. I protested and begged her not to, so instead she insisted on giving it to me to take home. It was in fact a study for a portrait of one of her granddaughters. Later Mary carefully flattened the picture and had it framed.

In 2003 Mary and two women friends, Glenda and Sue, who had been in the same intake of students in the Bournville Foundation Course, decided to start up a small gallery in Harborne High Street, our local shopping centre, where artists in the region could exhibit and sell their work. They found an ideal place to rent in a small secluded square off the High Street. It was a two-storey building previously occupied by a retailer who evidently used the spacious upper floor to exhibit their produce, so it was easily adapted to show art, and with the ground floor offered an inviting gallery walk-through. Glenda's husband (also called David) and I were happy to finance the start-up of the gallery. Mary and her friends ran it successfully for three years, mounting quarterly exhibitions, including a Tom Phillips retrospective with his generous co-operation. They also diversified the gallery's activities to offer advice, instruction and materials to people keen to improve their art and craft skills, or interested in learning how to paint. They were helped in all these tasks by enthusiastic art student volunteers, who mounted their own exhibitions at the end of each year. But it was a demanding commitment for the three women because at least one of them had to be on duty when the gallery was open.

After three years, having achieved their initial aims of providing the West Midlands with a first-class commercial art gallery, and opportunities for local artists to exhibit their work, they decided to call it a day. Small independent art galleries in the provinces usually struggle to make a profit, and often close down for that reason; but by selling the unexpired portion of their lease to another firm anxious to move in, Mary, Glenda and Sue broke even on the whole enterprise, which was the least they deserved, and very satisfying. For them it had been a rewarding and memorable experience, from which they had learned a lot.

To our great pleasure our son Christopher unexpectedly revealed a talent for art when he was in his forties. The community in which he lived had an art and craft facility, and one of the staff took him under her wing, encouraging him to paint, mainly in the medium of gouache, and sometimes acrylic. Nearly all his work was based on pictures or photographs but he treated them in a boldly personal style that used colour and outlining to great effect. His favourite artist is Van Gogh. Birds were a favourite subject, and we first realised what a gift he had when he produced a perky robin which the Down's Association adopted for its Christmas card that year. Later we became involved with an internet venture called Heart and Sold, started by the mother of a Down's child to encourage others who showed interest, to take up art and sell their work. This led to several exhibitions in different parts of the UK, including one in a gallery near London Bridge where Chris sold his painting of a Tawny Owl for a substantial price. He also accepted commissions from relatives and friends. All this was very good for his self-esteem.

10

After the failure to mount a production of *The Writing Game* in New York, I did not anticipate that there would be any more theatrical interest in that play, but I was wrong. In January 1996 I received a letter from a man in Paris called Armand Eloi, who introduced himself as the director of a small theatre company in which he sometimes also acted himself. He and his wife had discovered some of my novels in English editions in Holland and enjoyed them, but were not aware that I had written a play until they came to London after Christmas 1995 for a short holiday. They spotted a copy of the Secker edition of *The Writing Game* in the window of Waterstones in Garrick Street, and purchased it. Armand was much taken with the play and asked for my permission to translate it with a view to getting it produced in Paris, proposing to show it to a well-known Comédie Française actor who he thought would make a great Leo. I replied that I would be very pleased to see the play produced in France, but that he would have to speak first to Suzanne Sarquier, who owned a theatrical agency in Paris and acted as Curtis Brown's sub-agent for drama in France.

I mentioned that I was going soon to Cergy-Pontoise, a 'new town' situated about twenty miles north-west of Paris, to attend a rehearsed reading of *The Writing Game* in its community theatre. The Director had visited its Birmingham equivalent in the MAC (Midlands Arts Centre) the previous year, and I had met him on that occasion. He was interested in *The Writing Game* when I told him about it, and said he would like to incorporate a rehearsed reading in a literary festival he was directing in Cergy-Pontoise in May. I agreed, partly because I thought it would be a good opportunity to see Armand Eloi, who agreed to join me there. The reading was to be done in English, mainly by English-speaking actors recruited for the purpose. They worried during rehearsals that the audience would find the dialogue difficult to follow, and grow weary at the play's length. I shared their misgivings, but in the event the audience were determined to enjoy themselves, laughing a lot and applauding enthusiastically, which was kind of them because it was an imperfect production.

I met Armand at the theatre before the show and he turned out to be a very striking young man, tall, broad shouldered and handsome, whom one could imagine holding the stage in a historical drama. Belgian by nationality, he was brought up in an agnostic family, but educated at a Franciscan school and became interested in Catholicism, which was one reason why he was drawn to my novels. He headed a small troupe of actors with whom he toured plays, mainly in the Bordeaux area, and recently he had directed a play by Mario Vargas Llosa, the Peruvian novelist and Nobel Prize winner, who had praised the production. Armand was joined by his charming wife, Béatrice, who had recently had her first novel accepted for publication. They both spoke excellent English.

The following day I spent several more hours chatting to Armand. He had already translated *The Writing Game* and handed me a copy of the text, neatly printed and bound. He thought it should not be put on at a subsidised theatre of the kind he usually worked in, but at a commercial theatre in Paris, where there was an audience for a sophisticated literary play. He had already had a meeting with Suzanne Sarquier, and boldly asked her for temporary exclusive production rights in the play. Suzanne must have been impressed because she gave him three months to put a production together or demonstrate a realistic prospect of doing so. I was impressed with Armand myself. He seemed to me completely honest and sincere as well as highly intelligent, and I was very willing to let him try to get my play staged, though he admitted that it would only happen if we could attract a 'star' to perform in it. (How many times had I heard that before . . . ?) This was the beginning of a long collaborative friendship which, like most of my experiences in the world of theatre, fluctuated between hope, frustration, euphoria and disappointment.

Armand had asked me when we were in Cergy-Pontoise if I was writing another play, and I told him I had an idea for one. The subject was the journalistic interview, and its central scene was an encounter between a writer and a journalist. This was a kind of reporting which originated in the USA in the later nineteenth century, and was imported to Britain in the twentieth, where it was viewed with some suspicion at first, but became increasingly popular as a way of reporting on notable new books and work in the other arts, communicating the character of a novel or play or any other artefact not by objective description but in a face-to-face dialogue with the person who created it. This approach was directly opposed to T.S. Eliot's assertion in 1922 that 'poetry is not the expression of personality but an escape from personality', a statement designed to discourage biographical interpretations of his work. Other early modernist writers also cultivated 'impersonality'. James Joyce's alter ego, Stephen Dedalus, asserts in *A Portrait of the Artist as a Young Man*: 'The artist, like the God of creation, remains within or behind or beyond or above his handiwork, invisible, refined out of existence, indifferent, paring his fingernails.' At that time such writers did not as a rule give interviews to journalists. Henry James made an exception when he agreed to be interviewed for an American newspaper in order to support US intervention in the First World War, but he insisted on rewriting the journalist's copy so thoroughly that it became his own work.

It was not until after 1953, when a group of American editors based in Paris started a magazine called *The Paris Review*, and persuaded a number of distinguished writers, including T.S. Eliot, to collaborate in a series called 'The Writers' Workshop' in which they answered questions about their creative methods, that the journalistic interview became accepted as a serious form of critical discourse. Meanwhile, at a more popular cultural level, interviews with celebrities and interesting newcomers in the arts became, and have remained, staple features of newspapers, magazines, radio and television; and the face-to-face interview on-stage has been the favoured method for authors to present their work at literary festivals.

A social historian, author of several highly praised books about the changing state of Britain over several decades before and after the millennium, was asked towards the end of his life what was the most significant development of all in that period. He replied without hesitation that it was the growing importance of publicity in every area of human endeavour. He was surely right, and it affected literature and the arts as well as other kinds of occupation. MacGibbon & Kee, the publisher of my first novel, *The Picturegoers*, did not have a publicity department – my editor took care of that business, such as it was – but now it is a key department of any substantial publishing house, and setting up interviews for authors of new books is one of its most important functions.

In the 1990s a journalist, Lynn Barber, contributed a series of interviews with well-known persons in the arts and other spheres of public life to *the Independent on Sunday*, a companion paper to the daily *Independent*. These articles caused something of a sensation because instead of adopting the usual ingratiating and deferential manner of interviewer to interviewee, she highlighted negative aspects of their self-presentation. One typical case was an interview with a well-known male actor who received Lynn Barber wearing jogging trousers and, she reported, was 'playing pocket billiards' with their contents throughout the interview. Sometimes her subjects, having misgivings after the interview, would phone her and ask if she would delete or emend something they had said, and Lynn would blithely quote these interventions in her article.

How did she get away with it, one wondered, and how did she go on finding subjects willing to expose themselves to her scorn? The answer had to be the cynical maxim, 'There's no such thing as bad publicity'. That is not entirely true of course – really shameful behaviour can destroy a career – but presumably there are people willing to risk being mocked rather than forgo an opportunity to see a featured article about themselves, with photographic portrait, in a newspaper with many thousands of readers.

Reading Lynn Barber's articles made me think of the interview as an event which both parties are trying to control, with different and sometimes opposing motives. This made it an inherently dramatic situation, and I began to develop a story which would explore its possibilities in a play.

Two men who were close friends at university nourished literary ambitions which had different outcomes. Sam became a successful writer of screenplays for film and television. Adrian had a promising early career as a novelist which later fizzled out, and he retired to a cottage in Sussex with his wife Eleanor, making a modest living from occasional journalism and compiling anthologies. Both men were attracted to Eleanor when they were students, and Eleanor equally to each of them, so at that time they formed an inseparable threesome which was ostensibly platonic, but shared hidden secrets. After their graduation Eleanor married Adrian, while Sam became famous and wealthy, but less fortunate in marriage. He still sees his old friends occasionally, at long intervals.

The play consists of two acts. One Sunday morning in late summer Sam turns up unexpectedly at the cottage, breaking his journey to Gatwick for a flight to Los Angeles. He complains bitterly at being done over by a notoriously acerbic journalist, Fanny Tarrant, in that day's *Sunday Sentinel*, which Adrian and Eleanor have been reading and discussing over their breakfast in the first scene of the play. Discovering that Fanny had recently approached Adrian for an interview, Sam presumes it was to gather background information about himself, and persuades Adrian, against Eleanor's advice, to agree to see her and then 'write a piss-take profile of Fanny Tarrant for one of the other papers', thus giving Sam his revenge. This 'sting' does not however work as planned.

In the second scene of Act One Fanny comes to the cottage, from which Eleanor has absented herself, to do the interview – which turns into a verbal fencing match that Adrian wins by challenging Fanny to join him in the sauna he has installed in his back garden. Eleanor returns unexpectedly to the cottage, and is upset to find the pair in a compromising position, wearing bathrobes. Adrian makes himself scarce, and Fanny takes advantage of the situation to draw from Eleanor, and covertly record, some prejudicial information about him. The second act begins some weeks later with Sam arriving unexpectedly at the cottage in the early morning on his way back from Los Angeles, to find that the marriage of Adrian and Eleanor is in crisis. Adrian is behaving very badly to Eleanor, and Sam becomes her confidant and protector. The two men fall out.

For some time I was uncertain how to end the play. Obviously Fanny had to return to the cottage and contribute somehow to the resolution of the plot – but how – and why? I decided that she has just discovered that she is the natural child of Eleanor by either Adrian or Sam – uncertain who it was because Eleanor slept with both of them in their student days – and she comes to the cottage to announce this fact, bringing about a reconciliation between the two men. I showed a draft script to Bill Alexander and he thought it would work, but I was not convinced. I asked David Edgar to read the play, and when his first question was, 'Are we supposed to believe this ending?' I knew I would have to find a better one.

It was September 1997, and the death of Diana, Princess of Wales, together with her lover Dodi Fayed, in a car crash in Paris on the 31st of August was still fresh in most people's minds, as was its sequel – the thousands of spontaneous floral tributes, the tensions in the Royal Family, the dramatic funeral watched by millions on television, etc. etc. Mary and I normally took little interest in Diana's life, and were surprised by how affected we were by her death. But I was interested in the public response as reported in the media. It seemed to me that something like a national catharsis was taking place, epitomised by a man I heard on a radio phone-in programme, whose wife had recently died from cancer. They had been happily married for forty-four years and he loved her dearly, but he shed more tears for Diana than he did for his wife. He sounded puzzled but not embarrassed making this confession.

The more sophisticated members of the fourth estate were sceptical of the significance of such behaviour, and inclined to dismiss it as a temporary phenomenon exploited by the mass media, but I thought it was authentic. At breakfast one morning soon after the event, Mary read out to me a magazine article by a young female journalist expressing regret for a snide article she had written about Diana which was published just before the fatal accident, and to her own surprise as well as mine, Mary shed some tears of sympathy. I immediately imagined Fanny Tarrant in such a situation, feeling regret and remorse for something derogatory she had written about Diana which was due to be published on the very day of her death. I knew that to incorporate this material in my play would be very risky, inviting accusations of opportunism and bad taste. Nevertheless I had a hunch that it could be a *coup de théâtre* to which an audience at this time would relate, if I could find a plausible way to bring Fanny back to the cottage early on the Sunday morning when the news broke – news that the occupants of the cottage, Adrian, Eleanor and Sam, have not yet heard. I set to work accordingly.

I showed the new ending to Tony Clark, who cautiously approved it, and the completed script to Bill Alexander who gave it the green light, subject to agreed rewrites. In November there was a private reading of the play by actors in the Rep's production of *Julius Caesar*, and a discussion afterwards in which some expressed doubts about the introduction of Diana's death into the play. But Bill kept faith with it – to my great relief, because I thought it was so much stronger than the denouement of the previous draft.

I had not yet decided on a title for the play, which had to be announced in the Rep's forthcoming programme. I hesitated between *The Naked Truth* and *Home Truths*, and eventually settled on the latter. Unfortunately we discovered, too late, that a new play called *Home Truths* had been toured in England in the previous year, an oversight that was all the more embarrassing because the author was Rosemary Friedman, a novelist and essayist as well as a playwright, who had been a colleague of mine on the Society of Authors Management Committee in the past. I was unable to contact her at this juncture because she was in Thailand, but her agent thought she wouldn't mind the duplication because there were no future plans for her play, and Rosemary later confirmed this. In due course she came to see my play at the Octagon, which she enjoyed, and we remained friends.

The play had been scheduled for production in May 1998, but it was brought forward to February to fill a gap left by the late cancellation of another play. This was regrettable because it meant that every stage of the production had to be completed with insufficient time available. Casting in particular was a nightmare, with several actors who had expressed interest dropping out at the last minute, casting a cloud of anxiety over my Christmas, and the process was completed just three days before rehearsals *had* to start, early in the New Year. Fortunately, someone in the Rep's casting office thought belatedly of sending the play to Margot Leicester, a well-known actress, and offering her the part of Eleanor. She was available and accepted, to my relief – and then delight, when I learned that she was the wife of David Thacker, who had directed several of Shakespeare's plays for the RSC at Stratford, and several of Arthur Miller's plays in the West End, before he became the artistic director of the Bolton Octagon.

I had never met either of them at this point, but David had congratulated me on *Therapy* about a year earlier on a postcard written during a transatlantic flight, for which I thanked him, and I discovered that they were both fans of my other novels. I was sure this explained why Margot quickly accepted the part of Eleanor, in spite of knowing she would be paid at provincial rep rates and that it would entail a lot of wearying travel between London and Birmingham, which as the mother of several children she could well do without. She played Eleanor superbly and inspired the rest of the cast. It turned out that she and Brian Protheroe, who was cast as Adrian, had acted together often in the past, and this was helpful to the bonding process which every production requires.

We attracted a lot of advance publicity for our show. BBC radio sent someone from its main arts programme, *Kaleidoscope*, to interview me, and BBC2's equivalent, *Late Review*, sent a team to film a scene from the play to insert in their coverage. I agreed to be interviewed by Jeremy Paxman on *Newsnight* by two-way transmission immediately after the first night performance. The reason for this amount of attention was probably that the word had gone round that the play was in some respects a satirical take on contemporary journalism.

*

The Rep's first nights, known as Press Nights, were always on a Tuesday, with two previews. The first of these was on the preceding Friday, and my scribbled notes on it were '*First scene drags. Ending works. Airplane noises intrusive. Cut them. Jilly Cooper present as Bill's guest, also Fay Weldon. They seemed to enjoy themselves.*' The second preview was on the Saturday evening, and by custom free to families and friends of the actors and the Rep's staff, so it was well attended by an enthusiastic audience who filled three quarters of the vast auditorium, and the actors drew confidence from them. The front of house staff had been instructed to ask members of the audience as they left the theatre at the end of the evening if they had enjoyed it, and reported unanimously: 'The audience loved the play.' I was very encouraged, and looked forward to the Press Night.

Then fortune turned against us. At about 6 p.m. on Press Night, Tuesday the 13th of February, I had a call from Leah to say that she and a party of London critics were held up on their train at Coventry station because of trouble further up the line. Panic! What to do? Bill and his staff decided to make an apologetic announcement that the play would be delayed by thirty minutes, and fortunately the London party arrived not much later than that. The audience was less responsive than at the previews, which was not surprising, but it was warmly applauded at the final curtain, and I was in an upbeat mood when I was interviewed by Jeremy Paxman outside the theatre. He grilled me about the play in his usual style, but I can't remember the conversation, except that he ended by saying, 'Well, you have certainly rattled the cage,' which I interpreted as a reference to the media, and took as a compliment.

I had a meal with Leah afterwards, and she told me frankly that she didn't think there was much chance of the play transferring to London. This was something of a downer, but she was always completely honest in commenting on my work, and the early reviews tended to confirm her opinion. To move a new play from a provincial theatre to the cultural capital requires the lure of a bundle of rave reviews. For *Home Truths* there was one rave, in the *Daily Mail*, and favourable ones in the *Telegraph* and the *Birmingham Post*, but it was panned in *The Times* and the *Independent*. The *Observer's* critic was dismissive and the *Sunday Times* scornful. Only one London producer, Michael Codron, came up to Birmingham to see the play and said some nice things about it, but did not offer to produce it.

The last person of note to see the production was Lynn Barber, who had evidently heard that she had in some way inspired it, and decided to see for herself what it was like. When I heard that she had booked a seat for a mid-week matinée, no doubt so that she could return to London comfortably on the same day, I was disappointed, because these performances were not well attended at the Rep and it would be difficult for the actors to generate much of an atmosphere in that vast space. Lynn, however, wrote a brief but kind piece in the *Independent* which concluded, 'I enjoyed my matinée at the Birmingham Repertory Theatre. Now there's a sentence I never thought I would write.'

As far as I know *Home Truths* was the first work of fiction to contain substantial reference to the death of Princess Diana. It continued to have a life in different forms and venues, especially in France. When Secker & Warburg published the play early in 1999 I sent a copy to Françoise Pasquier, then my editor at Rivages, simply as a gift, thinking that she might be entertained by it, and she wrote back to say she thought it was wonderful and wanted to publish a French translation. I was not in favour because most readers are repelled by the format of play texts unless they are keen theatre-goers. However I had been thinking idly that one day I might try converting the play into a novella, so I wrote to Françoise to suggest this – and she jumped at it. Geoff Mulligan and others at Secker were also keen when I put the idea to them, and contracts were drawn up. It was a very enjoyable writing experience – the easiest I ever had, because the construction of the story, which for me is always the most difficult part of writing a novel, had already been done, and only needed to be fleshed out – for example, in the character of Fanny's boyfriend, Creighton, who is a mere off-stage name in the play, and the relationship between them.

There are numerous plays based on works of prose fiction, but the reverse kind of adaptation, turning a performed play into a novel or novella is rare; though Henry James wrote two short novels, *The Outcry* and *The Other House*, based on plays he had written but was unable to get produced. My novella was published by Secker in 1999 as *Home Truths* in an elegant paperback format, with a cover design based on a rough sketch of my own – which I liked so much that I had postcards made from it. It had modest sales in the UK, while the Rivages edition, translated by Suzanne Mayoux and entitled *Les Quatre Vérités*, sold 90,000 copies in its first year. In France, telling someone 'four truths' about themselves is a proverbial expression for making them aware of their imperfections.

Suzanne Sarquier admired my play and was determined to get it staged in Armand Eloi's translation, for which they adopted my alternative English title, *The Naked Truth*. Suzanne eventually secured a production for *La Vérité Toute Nue* in January 2007 at the Salle Popescu, a small space like the Birmingham Rep's Studio, built into the famous Théâtre Marigny just off the Champs Elysées. It had a strong cast and a well-known director, and I went to Paris to meet them and to attend the first night. Armand had explained to me that new plays in Paris normally had no interval and must take not more than one hour forty minutes to perform. This has since become an increasingly popular format for plays in Britain, but was then uncommon. Poor Armand had a tough time reducing my text to the required length. He managed it with my co-operation, but it seemed to me that the actors, a very enthusiastic and talented group, had to rush through the play to its disadvantage. They called me up on to the stage at the end and I took a bow with them. The play received excellent reviews, but the box office figures were disappointing, which Suzanne attributed to the fact that a presidential election was looming and Parisians were devoting their evenings to watching television coverage of the campaign. A real success with a stage play continued to elude me.

Some years previously I had become acquainted with a remarkable man who was similarly driven by the desire to write plays and see them performed. For both of us drama was one of several kinds of creativity which we practised, but in his case they were much more diverse. He was Carl Djerassi, and we first met at the Frankfurt Book Fair in October 1992, both being guests of our Swiss German publisher, Gerd Haffmans, who in that year published German translations of my novel *Nice Work* and of Carl's autobiography, teasingly entitled *The Pill, the Pygmy Chimps, and Degas' Horse.*

Born in 1923, Carl was a Viennese Jew who emigrated to the USA as a teenager with his mother in 1938, just in time to escape Hitler's Final Solution. He worked his way up through the American educational system to become an academic scientist, specialising in Chemistry, and rose rapidly in his profession. In 1949 he was invited to head a research team in a little-known pharmaceutical company in Mexico called Syntex, where he discovered how to synthesise the constituents of the contraceptive pill, which was approved for use in 1960. The importance of this discovery and its effects on human life, especially for women, cannot be exaggerated. By shrewdly investing in the company's stock and acting as an executive in its subsidiaries, Carl made himself a rich man. He did not retire from academic life however, but became a professor of Chemistry at Stanford University in California, noted for his innovative courses and the recipient of many distinguished awards for his research. But he was also devoted to the arts, and spent much of his wealth on them in different ways. He built up a collection of Paul Klee's work and gifted it eventually in two equal parts to museums in San Francisco and Vienna. With the proceeds from selling another collection of modern art, he converted a ranch he owned on the California coast into a retreat for artists of all kinds as a memorial to his daughter, a sculptor who took her own life, which was without doubt the most painful event in Carl's life.

Gerd Haffmans had booked us into the same hotel in Frankfurt, so we walked together to the site of the Book Fair. We had not met before, but Carl had written a letter to me once years earlier, though we must have forgotten it at the time. I recalled it myself only when I was preparing this book and came across a short letter from Carl in my files, about *Small World*, published in the USA in 1984. He was reading it on a long flight to an academic conference, and laughing so much that a stewardess became alarmed and asked him if he was feeling unwell. This made him laugh even more, with tears rolling down his cheeks, and he could only respond by pointing speechlessly at the book. He wrote to me, care of my publishers, to thank me for the entertainment my novel and this incident had given him.

We were glad of each other's company at the Book Fair, which can be a rather alienating experience for authors. It is a trade fair, not open to the public. The huge airless halls, their miles of aisles filled with publishers' stalls displaying thousands of books in every language, induce a kind of nausea, even despair. How could any individual book be noticed in this sea of print, one wondered? The publishers and agents are busy making deals all day, so there is not much for invited authors to do, except give the occasional press interview and have their photos taken, though Gerd ensured that we were invited to drinks parties and enjoyed some good meals.

Nice Work was the first of my books he published. My agents and their German sub-agent had been dissatisfied with the way other German publishers had handled the earlier ones, and recommended that we offer *Nice Work* to Gerd, and he accepted it enthusiastically. I looked forward to meeting him in person in Frankfurt, and was not disappointed. He was big in stature and in personality: genial, generous and good humoured, a real bookman, a collector as well as a publisher, an enthusiast who took pride in producing books that were a pleasure to handle as well as to read. He managed his company in Zurich with a small and dedicated team. The pages of his edition of *Saubere Arbeit* (1992) are still white today, while those of the Secker first edition of *Nice Work* are yellow at the edges. At this time Secker belonged to the Reed group of publishers, which meanly refused to spend money on acid-free paper.

Gerd had published books by Carl before any of mine, including his first novel, *Cantor's Dilemma* in 1989, which by happy chance I had read before we met. During a recent visit to Cambridge Mass., a Harvard professor had recommended it to me as an excellent academic novel which, unusually, was about scientists, not specialists in the humanities. I bought the Penguin edition of *Cantor's Dilemma* in Harvard Square and found it both entertaining and instructive. Professor Cantor is a microbiologist who has a theory about what causes cancerous tumours, and a burning ambition to win a Nobel Prize. He employs a research assistant to do an experiment which appears to confirm the theory . . . but did the assistant fake the result? That is the nub of the plot, but what continues to hold the reader's attention is the convincing evocation of the professional lives of scientists. I brought the novel home with me and passed it to my daughter Julia, who was then a research fellow in Microbiology at Birmingham University, and she said it was absolutely on the nail about the milieu it described, especially the power relations between senior and junior staff, and the delicate matter of giving individuals appropriate credit in the publication of collaborative work. When I told Carl of her comments he sent her an inscribed copy of his autobiography.

In 1985 Carl married Diane Middlebrook, also a professor at

Stanford. Her field was English and American Literature, and she was the author of a remarkable biography of the poet Anne Sexton and other books about American women poets. They were very different types, physically and temperamentally. Carl was small in stature, intense and Jewish. He limped, having had a damaged knee joint fused so that he could continue to walk – and ski. Diane was tall, calm, graceful and probably from a WASP background. It was not surprising that he struggled for several years to persuade her to marry him. They lived together for a time, but she left him for another man at one point, and he released his anger and jealousy in a book of poems in free verse entitled *A Diary of Pique*. It is surprisingly effective considering it is the only book of poetry he published, and it was highly praised in the *Hudson Review*. Eventually Diane capitulated to his tireless wooing, and married him. They occupied an apartment which spread over an entire floor of a high-rise building with a priceless view over San Francisco Bay and the Golden Gate Bridge, but both of them were attracted to the cultural life of London, especially its theatres, and Carl bought a London home where they spent several months of every year between spring and autumn.

It was a spacious flat in Maida Vale on the second floor of a terraced town house in a cream-stuccoed crescent, which had a large balcony at the back overlooking a private park shared by occupants of the crescent. Every summer, on or near American Independence Day, Carl and Diane held a large and lavishly catered party for friends and people in the arts, in collaboration with Elaine and English Showalter, another American academic couple whom Mary and I knew well. They too loved London and had a small flat there. Mary and I were regularly invited to these parties, and looked forward to them.

There was a certain *quid pro quo* entailed: namely a moral obligation to go to see the plays which Carl wrote in those days, which were produced (almost certainly funded by Carl himself) and performed by good professional actors for short runs in small London theatres. This was not an onerous duty, and was usually rewarding. Carl had successfully experimented with drama as a teaching tool at Stanford, getting his students to explore issues in science and applied science in dramatised dialogue, and the majority of his own plays had scientific themes, often derived from his own research interests. A subject of some importance and complexity – for instance, the ethical and interpersonal consequences of new techniques of *in vitro* fertilisation, or what constitutes an original discovery in science – was discussed and debated from various points of view, and the audience were challenged to make their own judgements about the issue. In later work Carl branched out into other areas of culture, notably in *Four Jews on Parnassus: a Conversation* (2008) a double dialogue between four famous Jewish intellectuals, Walter Benjamin, Theodor Adorno, Gershom Scholem and Arnold Schönberg. Carl more than once described the liberation he felt in escaping the constraints of scientific expository prose, in which the first person pronoun is taboo, and in the Preface to *Four Jews* he wrote: 'In my former incarnation as a scientist over half a century I was never permitted, nor did I allow myself, to use direct speech in my written discourse. With very rare exceptions, scientists have completely departed from written dialogue since the Renaissance, when especially in Italy some of the most important literary texts were written in dialogue ... Galileo is a splendid case in point.' In many ways Carl's extraordinary versatility as a scientist, novelist, dramatist, teacher and patron of the arts, made him seem a modern reincarnation of the ideal Renaissance man.

Unfortunately he had a fatal weakness which was particularly damaging in a British social milieu which values modesty and understatement. He was without doubt the most egotistical person I have ever known. When Mary and I met up with him and Diane in London he would immediately begin to tell us what his latest project was, but I do not remember him ever asking me what I was working on. He wanted to convince others of the importance of his own work and had an insatiable appetite for reassurance on this score. In his play *Three on a Couch*, a bestselling author plans to fake his own death in order to read his obituaries, and Carl admitted that he longed to read his own obituaries, which he knew would be written and set in type well before he died, if he could only get his hands on them.

Diane was well aware of how Carl's egotism grated on other people, especially her English female friends, and did her best to distract them and restrain him. He was devoted to her, and shocked when she was diagnosed with cancer in 2000. For Diane herself it was devastating because she was embarked upon what she hoped would be her crowning literary achievement – a biography of the Roman poet Ovid, whose writings she loved. Apart from the fact that he was exiled from Rome by the Emperor Augustus, nothing is known about Ovid's life. She believed this licensed her to construct a biography intuitively from his writings and her own scholarly research into his social and cultural context. She carried on with this project in spite of her illness, and had two operations in the first few years of the twenty-first century, neither of which was successful.

Carl was devastated by her death in December 2007 and predictably reacted by committing himself to work harder than ever on his plays, revising and improving them and flying around the globe from one major city to another to supervise new productions. He also gave generous financial assistance to a project of Diane's family and friends to complete her book about Ovid, which was published in 2014 as *Young Ovid: A Life Recreated*, and was highly praised by reviewers.

Some years later Carl himself succumbed to cancer, and resisted the inevitable with all the resources he could muster, but one day in January 2015 I got a letter from him to say that the end was very near – and would I please write his obituary for one of the English newspapers. Wondering how to tactfully decline, I did not reply immediately, and two days later, on the 20th of January, he died, at the age of ninety-one, which relieved me of what would have been a difficult epistolary task. A few years earlier I had written at Carl's request an introduction to a Festschrift celebrating his career, published by a German university press in English. It was a sincerely complimentary piece, some 3000 words long, covering the remarkable range of his achievements, and I put a good deal of thought and work into it. I did not think I owed Carl another panegyric, and I was confident that plenty of other obituaries would be written by others much better qualified to appreciate his scientific achievements than I. But I was, and remain, very glad that I had known this extraordinary man, and his gracious and gifted wife.

11

In writing these memoirs I have tried to give them something like the cohesion and continuity of a novel, and they contain episodes, such as a visit to a foreign country, or writing and participating in the production of a play, which provided the material for an extended, self-contained story. But as time goes on, a busy life contains more and more heterogenous events which seem worth recording, but cannot be linked together into a smoothly integrated narrative. My main method of dredging up memories of the past in the composition of these books is to leaf through the letters I received, and copies of those I wrote myself, during the period I was writing about. I kept them in folders and ring binders, holding a year's accumulation of miscellaneous correspondence in roughly chronological order. The following memories were recovered from the files for the late 1990s.

In June of 1996 I was informed that *Therapy* had been shortlisted for the Italian Scanno Prize, named for the city in the Abruzzo which awarded it. This novel had been translated and published by Bompiani in 1995 with the title *La felicità è di questo mondo*, which my Italian translator Mariella Gislon told me means: 'Happiness Belongs to this World'. Unlike most of my foreign publishers, Bompiani have rarely used titles which are close to the English originals, usually preferring to invent their own which sometimes surprised me, as this one did. I presume it refers to the hero's and heroine's eventual decision to seize happiness in this life when the opportunity arises, rather than place their hope in any afterlife. I didn't complain about these enigmatic titles because Bompiani produced beautiful books with fascinating covers using work by the brilliant Italian artist Tullio Pericoli. The Scanno Prize had an eccentric rule: the winner was obliged to receive and take away the prize, worth US$ 42,000, in gold ingots. I wondered how you would get them through customs on the way home if you happened to win, but in fact I heard no more from Scanno, and was not troubled further with this question.

In August 1996 my father reached his ninetieth birthday, and I planned a lunch party to celebrate it. The venue I chose was Rules restaurant in Maiden Lane, conveniently near my flat, which describes itself as 'established in 1798, serving classic British food in Edwardian surrounds'. I thought Dad would approve of that ambience and cuisine, and he did. We were given an upstairs room where Edward Prince of Wales used to entertain his mistresses. It had a long table which suited our party of sixteen comfortably. It included our nuclear family, plus Danny Moynihan and his wife Julia, an elderly cousin of Dad's, and a former school friend of my mother and her husband. Christopher enjoyed the occasion as much as anyone, and a photograph survives in which he is giving an earnest speech in Dad's honour. I regret that I was too far down the table to hear and remember what he said.

*

In late 1997 the new British Library on the Euston Road was opened, replacing the Round Reading Room of the British Museum in Bloomsbury. It had been years in the building, with so many technical problems that the consequent delays became something of a scandal. But at last it was finished and I was among a party of writers and scholars invited to a private view of the new Reading Room. To veterans like me of the BM's concentric circles of spacious desks and luxuriously comfortable chairs spread out under its huge dome, the new low-ceilinged rectangular space, with its serried rows of austerely functional desks and chairs, seemed rather soulless, but provided with all the latest computerised aids to scholarship, and a pleasant café on the floor below, it became popular with users before long. Our visit to the building was covered by the press, and at one point I was asked by the photographers to stand on a step ladder against a background of bookshelves, brandishing a book in one hand. It appeared in *The Times* the next day, with my usually tight-lipped features transformed into an expression of hilarious celebration – entirely caused by Kathy Lette, notorious for her saucy humorous writing, who was standing out of sight behind the step ladder and goosed me just as the cameras flashed.

At about the same time that year I was made a *Chevalier de l'ordre des Arts et des Lettres*, an honour occasionally bestowed by the French Minister of Culture in Paris on writers of other nationalities whose work is especially appreciated in France. I was of course very pleased, especially as I was free to invite friends to the formal award of the honour at the French Institute in Kensington early in December, presided over by the Cultural Counsellor and Director of the Institute, Olivier Poivre d'Arvor. I realised with some apprehension that the occasion would require me to make a speech of thanks in French, in which I am shamefully incompetent. However, with Mary's help and coaching I composed and rehearsed a brief address which seemed to go down well, and the rest of the evening was highly enjoyable, with so many friends present, including both my English and French literary agents.

I had reached that time in my life and career when honours of this kind may come one's way. A few years earlier I had been invited in a letter from the Cabinet Office to accept an OBE 'for services to literature'. I knew nothing about the Honours system at that time, and had a vague idea that it was medieval in origin, but soon discovered that it was invented shortly after the First World War, probably in the hope of suppressing uncomfortable memories of that terrible conflict with a celebration of old-fashioned chivalry and patriotism. I learned that the initials CBE stand for 'Commander of the most excellent Order of the British Empire', OBE for 'Member of the most excellent Order of the British Empire', and MBE for that same formula with 'the most excellent' omitted. It was a class system like the categories of railway coaches in those days: First, Second and Third. Knighthoods, a few of which did have historic origins, trumped all. These titles are formally bestowed by the Monarch or other members of the Royal Family at Buckingham Palace.

Like many writers who receive such an invitation, I felt uneasy at the prospect of being adopted by this factitious scale of merit, with its close relationship to the social and political Establishment. Would acceptance be a psychological constraint on one's spontaneous freedom of expression? After some hesitation I decided to decline the honour. I did not regret it, and was relieved that I had done so when Malcolm Bradbury was appointed CBE in the New Year's Honours List of the same year. We were so often paired together in the public eye that if I had appeared in the list it would have seemed like an official ranking of my literary status beneath him, when in fact we regarded each other as equals. Mike Shaw, who was the agent of both of us, was indignant that no one concerned with the Honours List had perceived and prevented the possibility of such an interpretation. I congratulated Malcolm without telling him I had declined the OBE, and a few years later, in 1998, I was appointed CBE myself.

This time I accepted the invitation. It was a simple decision: having recently accepted a similar honour from the French state, it would have been insulting to decline one from my native country. The public announcement on New Year's Eve prompted a flurry of congratulations from friends and readers in January. The investiture was scheduled for March. One was allowed to bring three guests to the ceremony and I thought that Mary, Dad and Chris would find it an interesting experience. Accordingly I ordered the morning dress traditional for these occasions (black tailcoat, grey waistcoat, dark trousers with a discreet stripe) from the Covent Garden Moss Bros., and booked a car to pick up Mary, Chris and myself at the flat in Charing Cross Road where we would have spent the night, going on to pick up Dad in Brockley, and then proceeding to Buckingham Palace for the investiture. Unfortunately, the magnificent chamber where these events normally took place was undergoing repairs and the spectators were seated in a less impressive and slightly scruffy space. And because we had arrived in a flustered state with little time to spare before the ceremony began, and I was seated separately from my family, Dad was not given a chair at the front with a good view which he had been promised on account of his age, and was unable to see or hear much of what was happening. It was my fault for underestimating the time required for the car journey, and a mistake that I still find painful to recall.

I received the medal from Queen Elizabeth. I had been briefed like all the candidates that day on how to conduct myself: don't attempt to shake hands with Her Majesty; address her as 'Ma'm' (rhyming with 'Sam'), let her speak first, and exchange a few words but not for long; when the medal has been pinned on to your chest, and the ceremony is over, bow and take several steps backwards before turning and leaving the area . . . I think that was the routine.

*

I met the Queen again several years later, during a big party at the Royal Academy given one summer evening to allow the extended Royal Family and their entourage to casually mingle with and chat to artists, musicians and writers. The handlers of the Royal Family were aware that the public view of them was that they lacked interest in the arts, and the occasion was designed to correct that perception. There was an excellent buffet, and a generous supply of champagne, of which I probably imbibed more than was prudent. I was chatting with a group of guests whom I knew in one of the Academy's galleries when the Queen entered the room with an escort who introduced her to us. I was impressed that she remembered me from the CBE investiture and said, 'Yes, we have met before.' I can't recall any more of the conversation that followed, but when I woke up later in my flat in the middle of the night and began to mentally replay the events of the evening, I had a sudden horrified recollection that I had unthinkingly extended my hand to shake the Queen's. Quite unfazed, she had shown no sign of surprise or displeasure, but took my hand and shook it. The little group I was in was not, I think, aware of any breach of etiquette on my part, and the encounter passed off pleasantly enough, but I felt a fool nevertheless for forgetting my briefing.

People tend to lose their self-possession when personally addressed by royalty. My father used to tell a story about an occasion when he was playing in the orchestra pit at a Royal Command Performance in the West End, probably in the early 1930s. When the show was over the musicians were lined up in one of the public areas for the Queen of that time to thank each of them with a few words. The man standing next to Dad, let me call him Ernie, was trembling nervously as she approached them. She praised the orchestra and asked Ernie if he had played in this theatre before. Making an effort to rise rhetorically to the occasion, Ernie stood to attention and exclaimed, 'Yes, O Queen!'

*

After my *faux pas* at the Royal Academy I thought I might have forfeited the chance of any subsequent invitation of the same kind, but some years later I was invited, with Mary this time, to a similar but smaller gathering at Buckingham Palace, a drinks party with canapés at which members of the Royal Family mingled with British writers in various genres. Princess Margaret appeared in the throng rather late and finding myself near her I introduced myself as a writer based in Birmingham, where she had consented to become a Patron of the Rep. A year or two earlier she had attended in this capacity a 'gala performance' of *The Threepenny Opera*, Bertolt Brecht and Kurt Weill's adaptation of John Gay's eighteenth-century classic *The Beggars Opera*, accompanied by a party of London friends in black tie and evening gowns. Mary and I were in the audience and watched them processing to their seats, chattering and laughing, no doubt having primed themselves with drinks at a reception beforehand, but they fell silent as the house lights went down, and remained so until the interval. When I reminded Princess Margaret of this occasion she gave me a black look, said, 'I remember it well. I think it was the worst evening of my life,' and moved off.

I was not surprised, for Margaret was known to have a sharp tongue, and that *Threepenny Opera* was one of the weakest productions I had seen in the Rep's main house. Although it is probably the most popular item in the Brecht–Weill repertoire, Brecht's plays are never easy to produce, and I wondered at the time why the Rep had chosen it for their Patron's visit. I discovered later that it had been the only vacant date in Princess Margaret's calendar, so the Rep was unable to offer another play from the season's programme. The cast were intimidated by the occasion, and the actress who played Polly Peachum, the most attractive character in the play, was plainly traumatised by the responsibility she felt and it affected her singing as well as her acting. The first half dragged, and Mary and I agreed we couldn't bear to sit through the second, so we crept out of the theatre in the interval, watched reproachfully by a member of the house staff, and went home to watch the TV coverage of that year's Booker Prize banquet.

To return to the drinks party at Buckingham Palace: wishing to escape from the conversational background noise of the main gathering which rendered my hearing aids almost useless, I wandered off into a succession of empty adjoining rooms hung with paintings, and stood in front of one of them. Prince Philip came in alone, as if he too was trying to escape, but courteously stopped to speak to me and we chatted for a few minutes. I told him I was a novelist, and wondered whether I dared to ask him if he had seen a cartoon in the *Sunday Times* the previous Christmas, which had greatly amused me. The newspaper's Books section in those days usually had a cartoon by an artist whose name I cannot remember or trace, and in this one the Queen and the Prince were depicted sitting together in a room in Balmoral Castle beside a large open packing case full of books and facing a log fire. A caption referred to a recent press release by an organisation supporting the book trade announcing that they had sent a hamper of new novels by British writers to the Royal Family as a Christmas present, and intended to make it an annual practice. Members of the Royal Family seldom expressed any interest in contemporary fiction, so this statement caused some amusement in literary circles, and had prompted the cartoon, which contained a pun on 'log'. A grumpy-looking Queen was urging Philip to 'Throw another Lodge on the fire, Philip,' and he was vigorously responding to the order, hurling a copy of *Therapy* through the air, pages flapping, with the title clearly legible on the cover. I thought that even if the Prince hadn't seen the cartoon he would be amused by my description of it, but before I could put this to the test a manservant entered the room and informed him that he was required elsewhere.

In the summer of 1998 Mary and I had a very enjoyable reunion with Lenny Michaels after a long interval – in Italy. He had married yet again, after a sometimes stormy relationship in Berkeley with a woman called Raquel whom I never met, but this time he found true happiness with his partner. Katharine Ogden was quite different from her predecessors, as we discovered in due course. A mature, attractive blonde with an upper-class background, she was a calm, confident, cultured businesswoman who managed an estate of holiday villas in northern Umbria. They had met in Berkeley and still spent half the year there, but lived in one of the villas from spring to autumn. It seemed an unpromising match given the history of Lenny's relationships, but it worked wonderfully well, as we discovered after he wrote encouraging Mary and me to visit them.

I arranged our summer holiday accordingly. We rented an apartment for a week in June, on the ground floor of the villa Lenny and Katharine occupied on the upper floor. I booked us into the Hotel Pelicano on the coast of Tuscany for the preceding week so that we could enjoy some sea bathing. It had an attractive situation, perched on a rocky promontory facing south-west. There was a heated swimming pool, and steps down to the ocean for the more adventurous. The accommodation was in cottages built on a steep slope above the pool, and staff brought your breakfast in boxes on motor scooters when you telephoned the kitchen. It was pleasant, but a little boring after a few days.

The nearest place with any life was Porto Ercole, a small fishing port, but its attractions were limited and we were glad to move on to our rendezvous with Lenny and Katharine. We broke our journey for one night in Orvieto, a city famous for its cathedral and the white wine produced in the surrounding vineyards. The Gothic cathedral's façade is an architectural masterpiece, and its splendour is matched by the art decorating the interior. We were enchanted by Orvieto, which was full of interest, but not as mercenary and crowded with tourists as more famous cities further north, and we would have liked to spend more time there, but we had to move on.

Umbria is a wilder, less inhabited region than Tuscany, but very beautiful. The estate managed by Katharine consisted of a number of separate houses of different sizes and shapes scattered over the top of a high hill with amazing views. I will never forget looking down into the valley below every morning and seeing it filled with thick white mist like a milky lake, which gradually evaporated as the sun rose in the sky.

On the day of our arrival Lenny was due to give a reading in the afternoon to a literary group in the nearest town, Umbertide, and he drove us and Katharine there to join the audience. I can't remember what he read, but it was probably one of the Nachman stories, as they were called when first collected and printed in 2007. These short stories are all centred on the character of Raphael Nachman, a solitary, ageing mathematician, and they are utterly different in style from the early writings that made Lenny's reputation. Those were written in a high octane prose, as if the words were sprayed from the muzzle of a machine gun, loaded with desperation, anger, violence, black comedy and transgressive sex. Nachman perceives the same world but in a much calmer, more reflective mode, puzzled rather than outraged by the vagaries of human behaviour he encounters. It is impossible to describe the extraordinary effect of such a seemingly passive and diffident character being employed as the point of view of every story. You have to read the texts for their spell to work on you.[1]

It is also impossible not to connect Lenny's 'late style' to his happy relationship with Katharine. Alas, it did not last long. A few years later a distraught Katharine told us that Lenny was seriously ill, and she was taking him back to the US immediately for hospitalisation. It seems that he experienced a catastrophic collapse of several vital organs at the same time, and he died in hospital in 2003, at the age of seventy. His reputation has grown steadily since

[1] *The Nachman Stories*, edited by Katharine Ogden, are published by Daunt Books in the UK.

then and his place in the history of twentieth-century American fiction is higher than it was in his lifetime. That has pleased his fans, though as Stanley Fish, who first introduced me to Lenny, remarked, with reference to him in one of his own *New York Times* columns, posthumous success is no compensation to a writer for years of struggle and disappointment.

12

How do novels come into being? Novelists often speak, or privately think, of 'getting an idea' for a new novel, but what does 'idea' mean in this context? By way of defining it, I say: a novel is a long answer to the question, *'What is it about?'* That is what any potential reader of a novel recommended by a friend, or displayed in a bookshop, will want to know, and they may get some notion of its content from the friend's answer or from the blurb on the book's jacket. But to grasp fully what it is 'about' you have to read the whole book, making provisional judgements and interpretations as you go along, and then condense and articulate your sense of its meaning and value when you come to the end. The author himself or herself will only find the long answer to the question in the course of writing the novel, which may be significantly different when it is completed from what they envisaged when they started it.

Most novelists begin by getting hooked on the story-telling power of prose fiction as readers, and then desire to emulate it as writers. This may entail some imitation of models, but not simple copying. The genre is well named: the story of a novel must have some novelty, and for that you need an 'idea' that will generate a variety of narrative possibilities as it grows, like cell division in biology. The originating idea might be inspired by your own experience, or by your observation of other lives, or a mixture of both. I gave an example in the first volume of my memoirs. In 1969 I returned from a six-month visiting professorship at the University of California at Berkeley with my head full of vivid memories and impressions, and was wondering how I could use them to write a novel different from those which already existed about British academics adjusting to the unfamiliar milieu of an American campus. Then I suddenly thought of their counterparts, the American academics who spent a term or year in a British university, often under some kind of exchange scheme between institutions on each side of the Atlantic. Nobody, as far as I was aware, had written a novel about one of those people, and I realised that *combining* two such narratives in a single novel, switching its focus back and forth between the two locations, could give an amusing picture of each culture seen through the eyes of two such visitors. That was the moment when I 'got the idea' for *Changing Places*.

This kind of discovery does not always derive from personal experience. It may be inspired by something one reads, as was the case with *Thinks . . .* , a novel I wrote long after *Changing Places*, published in 2001. I 'got the idea' for it in 1994 from a long book review by John Cornwell in the *Tablet*, the excellent Catholic weekly. Cornwell was born in 1940 and brought up as a Catholic by his devout mother. He entered a junior seminary at the age of thirteen with the intention of becoming a priest, but left the senior seminary abruptly just before he was due to take his vows, to study literature at Oxford and later Cambridge, where he became a Fellow of Jesus College and Director of an interdisciplinary forum called the Science and Human Dimension Project. He is a prolific author of books and journalism on a wide variety of subjects. His article in the *Tablet* which caught my attention was headed 'From Soul to Software', and it discussed two recently published books about human consciousness: *The Astonishing Hypothesis* by Francis Crick, the British scientist who, in partnership with the American biologist James Watson, discovered the molecular structure of DNA, and *Consciousness Explained* by Daniel Dennett, an American philosopher with a special interest in Cognitive Science and Artificial Intelligence.

As recently as 1989 Stuart Sutherland, Professor of Psychology at Sussex University, had written in the *International Dictionary of Psychology*, 'Consciousness is a fascinating but elusive phenomenon; it is impossible to specify what it is, what it does, or why it evolved. Nothing worth reading has been written about it.' But in the following year a paper published by Crick and Christof Koch declared that 'it is time to make human consciousness the subject of empirical study', and from then onwards it became an increasingly hot topic in the academic world. Hundreds of books and articles have been published on the subject in the last thirty-odd years, many of which are well worth reading. Most addressed directly or indirectly what the American philosopher David Chalmers called 'the hard question' in cognitive science: namely, how does a material brain produce the phenomenon of consciousness or 'mind'?

The hypothesis that Crick presumed would astonish most of his readers was that 'You, your joys and your sorrows, your memories and your ambitions, your sense of personal identity and free will, are in fact no more than the behaviour of a vast assembly of nerve cells and their associated molecules.' To him, to Daniel Dennett and most cognitive scientists, the human brain works like a computer endowed with enormous power and speed. Or as Stephen Pinker, an American psychologist in the same school of thought put it, more reductively: 'the mind is a machine, nothing but the on-board computer of a robot made of tissue'. There were affinities between these views and those of the logical positivist British philosopher Gilbert Ryle, whose famous pronouncement on the concept of mind was, 'There is no ghost in the machine', and the biologist Richard Dawkins, British author of bestselling popular science books, who maintained that Darwin's theory of evolution satisfactorily explained everything about how the world we inhabit came into existence without the agency of a transcendental Creator. He and like-minded writers were soon grouped together journalistically as proponents of 'the new Atheism'.

John Cornwell's thoughtful review in the *Tablet* of the books by Crick and Dennett, which I read as soon as I could get my hands on them, set me thinking about the challenge this new scientific work on consciousness presented to Christianity and other religions which share the belief that *homo sapiens* has a material body and an immortal soul. It was also challenging, it seemed to me, to the Enlightenment concept of the individual man or woman on which 'character' is based in the post-Renaissance novel: individual persons continually interpreting the world in which they grow up and conduct their lives, responsible for their actions, constantly adjusting and revising their hopes and desires according to their circumstances.

I began to think of writing a novel about this matrix of ideas and theories. On the face of it this was an absurd ambition, for I knew virtually nothing about science, cognitive or otherwise, having dropped badly taught physics and chemistry at secondary school as soon as I was free to do so. But consciousness – the ways individual human beings observe and react to the world they inhabit from moment to moment – was a phenomenon absolutely central to the novel of the last two centuries, the literary genre in which I specialised as a critic and writer of fiction; and when I started to read some of the many books about it by cognitive scientists of various kinds I found I could usually understand and profit from them.

It was an advantage to be an honorary professor at Birmingham University, which had a large and flourishing School of Computer Science. I contacted the head of it, Aaron Sloman, Professor of Artificial Intelligence and Cognitive Science, and asked him if he could give me some basic instruction in this subject area. He generously agreed and gave up some of his precious time to talk to me, and invited me to attend his weekly postgraduate seminars, which often had guest speakers. At first our private conversations were the meeting of two very different and mutually baffled minds, for he knew as little about writing novels as I did about computer science. But over time our relationship became easier, and he kindly invited and escorted me to a big international conference on the current state of consciousness studies which took place at Elsinore in Denmark – most appropriately since it was the home of Shakespeare's most consciousness-conscious hero, Hamlet. When Hamlet says 'conscience doth make cowards of us all,' he uses the word *conscience* to mean what we call consciousness in modern English, and what it has always meant in French.

At Elsinore I was identified among the conferees as a lone stray from the arts and humanities, and the object of some curiosity on this account. Perhaps at Aaron's suggestion I was invited to give my impressions of the event and views on the issues discussed, at the end of the last day of the conference. I put some notes together for a talk which I later developed and incorporated into the book I was planning to write. When I showed Aaron the completed text he gave me some helpful notes and took an interest in its fortunes, eventually speaking about it on Melvyn Bragg's radio programme, *Start the Week.*

In order to generate a novel from all this newly acquired information I needed a story. I conceived two main characters: a cognitive scientist, Professor Ralph Messenger, and a novelist, Helen Reed, who meet when she comes to teach a postgraduate course in creative writing for a semester at a new university in the Cotswolds, where Messenger is director of a research institute, the Centre for Cognitive Science. They are sexually attracted to each other but ideologically and ethically opposed. Helen is a lapsed Catholic still mourning the sudden death of her husband a year earlier, and she struggles to resist Ralph's efforts to seduce her. The story is told in three alternating narrative modes: Ralph's spontaneous recordings of his thoughts to generate data for his research; Helen's private journal; and an impersonal report of events in the present tense. I called the novel *Thinks . . .* , a word that appeared with an ellipsis in bubbles above the heads of characters in the comics I read as a child, to indicate that they were not speaking their thoughts aloud. One of Ralph's dictums is, 'We can never know for certain what another person is thinking,' and Helen believes that we read literary fiction partly for the illusion it creates of having access to the secret thoughts of others.

I researched and wrote *Thinks . . .* during the last three years of the century, years saddened for me by the deaths of three men who had greatly influenced and enhanced my own life in different ways. In November 1997 John Blackwell died suddenly and unexpectedly in his South London home, of pulmonary embolism. He was a habitual Gauloise smoker and drinker of beer and wine, sometimes to excess, but I was shocked, for he was only sixty, two years younger than me, and saddened because he had been the meticulous editor of my novels and a good friend ever since I became a Secker & Warburg author and collaborated with him in preparing *Changing Places* for publication in 1975. In my first memoir I described what a pleasure it was to work with him then and afterwards. I wrote an obituary for the *Independent*, and Malcolm, who had also been edited by John for almost as many years, wrote one for another paper.

John was a publisher of a kind by now virtually obsolete: a desk editor who devoted himself to editing, including the time-consuming business of copy-editing, rather than commissioning and acquiring new books. It is not the way to advance up the corporate ladder, but he was never personally ambitious. He simply cared passionately about publishing good books. He was a perfectionist, and since most writers of what is called in the book trade 'literary fiction' wish their work to be as near perfect as possible, his scrupulous editing was also valued by several well-known novelists not on the Secker & Warburg list. The letters he wrote to his authors and colleagues were legendary for their acuity, wit and erudition; and he excelled as a writer of those short, evocative and hopefully enticing descriptions of books known as 'blurbs'.

If John Blackwell's death was shockingly sudden, Malcolm's was the sad conclusion to a year of gradual physical decline and professional disappointment. In 1999 he complained increasingly of being short of breath after any exertion. This was eventually diagnosed as the symptom of a rare respiratory disease, which affected his mobility. He was knighted 'for services to Literature' in the New Year's Honours List – deservedly, considering not only his published work, but also the time and effort he had expended on frequent foreign tours for the British Council, and his successful management of the UEA creative writing programme. The honour was gratifying to Malcolm, Elizabeth and their two sons, but when I phoned to congratulate him he immediately referred to the lowering effect of anxiety about his lungs. A few months later it was thought prudent to convey him in a wheelchair through the passages of Buckingham Palace to be knighted by the Queen.

Malcolm had been working for some years on a new novel about the French writer Dennis Diderot, whose *Encylopedia* was the handbook of the eighteenth-century Enlightenment in Europe. He had been fascinated to discover that Diderot left Paris for several years, taking his private library with him, to join the court of Catherine the Great of Russia, and had written a novel called *Jacques the Fatalist*. It was modelled on *The Life and Opinions of Tristram Shandy, Gentleman* by the English writer Laurence Sterne, a work sometimes called 'the first antinovel' by modern critics, because Tristram is constantly, and comically, defeated in his efforts to give a coherent and complete account of his life. Malcolm was a devoted fan of Sterne, and drew on this matrix of connections to write a long, digressive, quasi-autobiographical, Shandian novel called *To the Hermitage.* He worked on it for several years and clearly hoped it would make a notable climax to his literary career. He was deeply hurt and disappointed when Secker & Warburg, the publisher of all his previous novels, showed no enthusiasm for To The Hermitage when he submitted it, and made no offer to publish it. John Blackwell was dead, and Tom Rosenthal had left Secker, disenchanted with the corporate publishing group to which it belonged, so Malcolm lacked strong support in the company. Picador, an enterprising, relatively new publisher of literary fiction, made an acceptable offer for the book and published it well in the spring of 2000, but the reviews were mixed, and some by younger critics were wounding. In spite of his poor health Malcolm insisted on committing himself to the full publicity programme now expected of novelists, touring their latest books around the bookshops and literary festivals, but he had to cancel some engagements. His lungs deteriorated further, and did not respond to the medication usually prescribed for his condition, which itself had serious side effects.

When I visited him in October of that year, he was confined to a bed which had been set up in his spacious ground-floor study. He looked ill and deeply depressed. He said to me, 'I'm beginning to think I'm not going to get over this.' I demurred of course, but I feared he might be right. Imagining how enviably healthy and happy I must seem to him, and how I would feel in his situation, I pitied him from the bottom of my heart. In the course of our conversation, as he recalled the disappointments and setbacks he had experienced that year, he uttered a sentence with a Shakespearian rhythm and resonance: 'I feel I am the most unfortunate of men.' He wasn't, of course, but the sentiment was entirely understandable.

Malcolm's condition rapidly deteriorated, and he died in hospital at the end of November 2000, with Elizabeth and their two sons at his bedside. The news was a shock to the literary world, because he had insisted that they should not broadcast the seriousness of his illness. There was a private funeral in a country churchyard, which Mary and I attended, and later a memorial service in Norwich Cathedral attended by more than 500 people, evidence of how sadly he was missed by readers in many different walks of life. I was one of several friends and former colleagues who spoke on that occasion. I concluded by saying: 'The great consolation we have for Malcolm's passing is that we can re-experience his character, and his life-enhancing sense of fun, through his books. But that is not the same, of course, as a living, breathing, laughing friend.' His capacity to generate laughter and appreciate it in others was perhaps the gift for which he was most loved, and mourned.

In October 1999 my father died, his health having been a cause of increasing anxiety to me for some years. After my mother's death in 1981, he continued to live alone at the house in Brockley, which had been my home from the age of one until I married. For many years he looked after himself competently, shopping and cooking, keeping the house clean with the aid of a loyal home help, and pursuing his own leisure interests, which included occasional day trips to Brighton to fish off the Marina sea wall. I visited him when business brought me to London, and he stayed with us for short breaks in Birmingham. One summer we took him and Christopher to Guernsey for a week's holiday, which he greatly enjoyed. But he was an independent and resourceful man, with several hobbies and interests, quite content to live at home on his own.

When Dad passed into his nineties, however, it became increasingly obvious that his mental faculties were deteriorating, and I was worried by the chaotic state of his kitchen and of the documents in his bureau desk. More and more evidence accumulated that he was suffering from mild dementia, and his GP confirmed this diagnosis. Mary and I discussed the problem, and agreed that we could not contemplate inviting him to live with us permanently. It was a harsh, perhaps selfish decision, but we knew this would have a catastrophic effect on our marriage. The amicable relationship between Mary and Dad was always a fragile one. We could make it work when he came to stay with us for short periods, but there were too many incompatible traits – temperamental, behavioural and cultural – in each of them to make a happy cohabitation possible.

Mary had already persuaded her mother, who was also in her nineties, to move into an Anchor House apartment in Hoddesdon, where she had spent most of her adult life. It offered comfortable accommodation for the elderly, and she felt happy and safe there until her death. The only solution I could see for Dad's vulnerability was to persuade him to move to Birmingham and take up residence in one of the care homes for the elderly that existed in our part of the city, so that we could meet easily and often. When I put this proposal to him, he shook his head sadly, and said that much as he enjoyed his occasional visits to us in Birmingham, he could not contemplate living permanently away from his own home and its surroundings. His GP told me his instinct was right, because old people depend on the cues of a familiar domestic environment to perform the ordinary tasks of living independently. But there came a point in time – perhaps when Mary and I saw traces of a frying pan fire on the kitchen wall above the stove – when we decided he could no longer live safely on his own.

Together we visited several care homes near our own house and found one which we thought would suit Dad. I managed to extract from him a reluctant promise to come up to Birmingham and have a look at it. This visit, however, had to be postponed until after we returned from a week-long excursion to Belgium and France already planned for the late summer of 1999. Our first destination was a care home in Namur, the historic city in Belgian Wallonia where my aunt Lu, the widow of my uncle John, had chosen to spend her last years. We were responding to her desperate plea that Mary and I should visit her one last time before she died. Conscious of how generously hospitable she had been to us in the past, I agreed to make the visit, and added to the trip a few days' break for ourselves on the Normandy coast. We took our car across the Channel and spent a couple of days with Lu in her care home, then drove to a small seaside resort in Normandy called Veules-les-Roses, chiefly distinguished for having the shortest river in France from source to the sea, where we enjoyed a pleasant and restful few days, staying in a small private hotel.

On the morning of our last day, we were packing our bags to leave for the journey home when I received a phone call from the mother of the Italian family who lived next door to Dad in Brockley – a kind lady who was a good neighbour to him. She told me he had suffered a stroke, and had been admitted to hospital. The details were troubling: apparently, he had collapsed on the floor in front of his TV when leaning forward to increase the volume. It continued to emit throughout the night and into the next morning, so loudly that the next-door neighbours investigated and saw Dad through the windows at the rear of the house, lying face down on the floor of the living room. They had broken into the house, called an ambulance, and told us that he was conscious and apparently uninjured, but had been taken to Greenwich Hospital.

It was fortunate that our bags were packed and we were ready to leave immediately. Dieppe was not far away. We took the ferry to Dover, and drove straight to Greenwich Hospital, where we found Dad in a cubicle in A&E waiting to be seen by a doctor. He was glad to see us, quite calm, perhaps mildly sedated, and not injured in any way. After the doctor had examined him he was given a bed on a ward, where I visited him frequently in the days that followed, helping the nursing staff care for him to the best of my ability, and returning to my flat each night, while Mary returned home to Birmingham.

Days lengthened into a week, and then another week. The doctors were concerned about Dad's declining strength and one of them consulted me about his future treatment. He was now unable to swallow food. He could be kept alive for an indefinite period by being transferred to another hospital and fed through a tube directly into his stomach, or they could make him as comfortable as possible and let nature take its course. I knew what I would choose if I were in that situation, but I did not feel I could make the choice for him. The next day, having returned to my flat after spending an afternoon beside his bed, when he was breathing stertorously with the aid of an oxygen mask, I received a phone call from the hospital in the late evening to say that he was not likely to survive the night. I left the flat immediately and took a cab to the hospital, where the ward sister told me with regret and sympathy that Dad had passed away five minutes after she phoned me.

Some readers of this book may have read my novel, *Deaf Sentence*, published in 2008, and will recognise in the above account of my father's last few weeks of life the source of the corresponding episode in that work of fiction. I do not know whether such a discovery makes the fictional narrative seem more, or less, interesting and convincing. Probably it depends on the character of the reader. The last pages of the novel also drew on my experience of arranging Dad's funeral and celebrating his life.

13

Thinks . . . was scheduled to be published in the first year of the new millennium. The approach of that rare chronological event had been anticipated globally with growing excitement, and also anxiety. It was feared that the world's computers, which were programmed to recognise dates only in the old millennium, would not function correctly in the new one. In spite of the assurances of experts that the problem could be fixed, theories and rumours circulated predicting that from Day One of the year 2000 we could expect airplanes to suddenly fall out of the sky and other modern processes dependent on computers to malfunction. I trusted that this threat would not affect the planned publication of my novel in March. Of course nothing at all happened.

The Islamist terrorist group Al Qaeda, however, had planned a spectacular catastrophe to make its mark on the new millennium. No one who was alive and awake on the 11th of September 2001, with access to television, will ever forget that day and its images of the twin towers in New York burning and collapsing, after two passenger planes hijacked by the terrorists were flown deliberately into the World Trade Center, killing nearly three thousand people.

The world had suddenly become a much more dangerous place, and our lives would never be the same.

It so happened that on 9/11, as that dreadful day came to be known, I was preparing to fly to America a few weeks later. Back in May I had accepted an invitation to give the Richard Ellmann Lectures at Emory University in Atlanta, Georgia, early in October 2001. Emory is a research university, richly endowed by the Coca Cola company which started up in Atlanta in the late-nineteenth century. It admits only postgraduate students and has built up an impressive collection of rare modern literary manuscripts in its library. Richard Ellmann was a distinguished American scholar and critic specialising in twentieth-century Irish literature, who moved with his family to Oxford in 1970 to become Goldsmiths' Professor in the University and a Fellow of New College. I described in *Writer's Luck* how I got to know him as a friend with whom I corresponded and met on occasional visits to Oxford. He retired as Emeritus Professor in 1980, but soon accepted a new appointment as Visiting Professor at Emory, where he was greatly appreciated. In declining health he returned to England, and died there in 1987. The Ellmann Lectures were founded in his memory, and I felt honoured by the invitation.

Professor Ron Schuchard, a veteran member of the Emory English Department, wrote to me: 'We wish to commission you to write and deliver three lectures on aspects of modern literature that are important to you at this time.' A substantial honorarium and all travel expenses were included in the invitation, and the lectures would be published for Emory by Harvard University Press. Ron described the Ellmann Lectures, the first of which had been delivered by Seamus Heaney in 1988, followed at yearly intervals by other distinguished writers and critics, as 'a major intellectual celebration, with all deep-south festivities including a famous pig-roast'.

I accepted the invitation and was looking forward eagerly to the occasion, especially as Mary was invited to accompany me. I was sure she would enjoy the trip, because Emory proposed to fly both of us to Atlanta in business class, and with that incentive I was able to persuade her. Georgia and its neighbouring states were a region of the USA that we had not explored in our travels across America in 1964–5. I thought we could add a week's holiday to the Emory visit, hire a car, and go to the South Carolina coast, or New Orleans, before returning home.

Alas, 9/11 put a stop to that plan, and cast a shadow over the one in place. Emory assured me that the lectures would go ahead as scheduled, and I confirmed my commitment to give them. Mary had been shocked by the attack on New York, like most people in Britain, but perhaps more deeply than the average watcher of the news, because she had lived happily for a year in America. To return there now, aware that further attacks might be launched in the near future, was a forbidding prospect. She said bravely that if I really needed her to accompany me, she would go, but her eyes said she would rather not. I didn't press her, and went to Emory on my own. It was fortunate that I did. As my plane was taxiing to the runway at Heathrow, it suddenly stopped and was surrounded by several cars. The aircrew opened a door to let down a set of steps, and a number of men in suits jumped out of the cars, boarded the plane, and went through it opening the overhead lockers, presumably checking for explosive devices. I thought later that Mary would have been alarmed by this incident at the very start of our journey, and I was glad she had not been exposed to it.

The Ellmann Lectures were open to all members of the University, and spread over a week with a day's break between them. I was free to choose my own subject. Having just finished *Thinks . . .* I did not hesitate for long. My head was still full of ideas about, and connections between, the phenomenon of consciousness and the literary novel as a genre, so I proposed 'Consciousness and the Novel' as my title. With *Thinks . . .* now off my hands and being prepared for publication at Secker & Warburg, I wrote my lectures. I called the first one 'Consciousness and the Two Cultures'. The latter phrase had been coined by the novelist C.P. Snow for a famous public lecture he gave in 1959, entitled 'The Two Cultures and the Scientific Revolution', arguing that in Britain the potential of science to change the world for the greater good had been stifled by the ignorance of science among people at the highest level of government, whose public school and Oxbridge education had been mainly based on the humanities. It was immediately attacked by F.R. Leavis in a dissenting lecture, starting a lively public debate which continued for several years.

I appropriated Snow's phrase in my first lecture to describe two opposing views of consciousness in contemporary culture. One was intuitive and drew on the arts and humanities for illustration and inspiration, and the other was informed by developments in cognitive science. They were frequently opposed to each other, but not irreconcilably so. I had recently read a remarkable novel by the American Richard Powers called *Galatea 2.2*, the core story of which is a wager about whether it is possible to build a machine that can pass an examination in English literature, and I used it to illustrate my theme. The second lecture was called 'First Person and Third Person'. Science is third person discourse, signalling its impersonality by banishing the pronoun 'I' from its publications. Writers of literature, whether in poetry or prose, are free to write in the first person or the third person, or to combine them in 'free indirect style' to render the unspoken thoughts of fictional characters. The third lecture was called 'Surface and Depth', and analysed the various ways in which prose fiction has represented the thoughts and emotions of characters in the modern era. I suggested that there had been a general shift of focus from psychological depth to behavioural surface during the first half of the twentieth century. (Compare Henry James and Evelyn Waugh, for example.)

The audience for the first lecture had seemed to me disappointingly small for the size of the auditorium, but the second was much better attended, and the third attracted nearly a full house. Ron Schuchard was delighted with the feedback he received from colleagues. The lectures had been a success, and I could relax. There were three swimming pools on the extensive campus, and I made use of the one most conveniently located for me. Ron ensured that I was never lonely, and initiated me into the ritual of the Pig Roast, which was his special responsibility. He took me to a market where all kinds of meat and offal were on display, and where we collected an enormous pig, split open and eviscerated, and watched it loaded on to a truck in what disturbingly resembled an open coffin. The carcass was then cooked very slowly over hot coals, checked by Ron at intervals in the night, and the meat at the barbecue the following evening was certainly delicious. Faculty and students mingled sociably around the tables and sipped wine. I noticed a girl wearing a tee-shirt with *YES I SAID YES* inscribed on it, a quote from the last line of James Joyce's *Ulysses*, where Molly Bloom recalls the moment when she yielded to Leopold's desire. At Emory, hooking up was obviously conducted at a high cultural level.

I shared other meals in the course of the week with members of the Emory faculty and academics from other universities, some of whom I knew personally, who had been invited to the lectures. Among them was Marjorie Perloff, the UCLA professor who had invited me to the 1978 MLA Convention in New York, and I thanked her for giving me the experience on which I drew for the closing chapters of *Small World.* That phrase still seemed a very appropriate name for the contemporary academic elite who kept meeting each other at scholarly gatherings around the world. Ruth Watt, the widow of Ian Watt, author of *The Rise of the Novel*, whom I had met only once, at Nice University when Ian was Visiting Professor there, greeted me at one of these agreeable dinners at Emory, having flown from Stanford in California to hear the lectures, and Tom Flanagan, the specialist in Irish literature at Berkeley when I was a visiting professor there in 1969, also turned up at Emory for the occasion.

Inevitably the conversation at meals and other social gatherings was still dominated by the events of 9/11 and their sequel. When I was driven from the airport through the suburbs of Atlanta I had noticed that most houses, from the humble to the luxurious, were flying the Stars and Stripes in a demonstration of patriotic defiance, and I was reminded that, as a Brit, I was an outsider who had not been subjected to the same deep shock as American citizens, and that I must always be mindful of this. I recall, at one of the meals, Marjorie Perloff, a clever and witty woman who was normally entertaining company, furiously denouncing the Cambridge classicist Mary Beard's recent remark in the *London Review of Books*, 'Some people think that America had it coming.' I thought it had been a tactless observation, to say the least, but I did not comment.

When *Thinks* . . . was published by Secker in the spring of 2001, it was favourably reviewed, and prompted an unusual number of letters to me from readers, several of whom expressed surprise that it wasn't shortlisted by the Booker judges. The letter that cheered me most was a very late one from Professor Randolph Quirk, who had lectured to us undergraduates at University College London in the 1950s on modern linguistics, before he rose in status to become the recognised supreme authority on spoken and written English in the UK. He wrote to me in March 2003: 'I've at last got round to reading *Thinks*, and David, I'm bowled over; it's just superb – compelling, clever, informative, cunningly crafted, well researched.' No tribute could have pleased me more.

The book did very well when published in France under the title *Pensées Secrètes* and was at the top of the bestseller lists there for several weeks. A few years later I received a letter from a Belgian director/actor/writer, Benoît Verhaert, previously unknown to me, asking for permission to adapt *Thinks* . . . as a play for two actors, based on the French translation of the novel, to be produced at

Théâtre Le Public, a well-known subsidised theatre in Brussels. He enclosed a rough, incomplete draft of his proposed play. It had never occurred to me that this novel, with its numerous characters and locations, could be adapted for the stage. But Benoît's proposal made me realise that it could be very effectively dramatised as a two-hander, without all the contextual detail of the novel. That could be stripped away without affecting the coherence of the narrative, which would unfold in monologues based on Ralph's recordings of his thoughts, and argumentative dialogues between him and Helen, of which there were many in the 'third person' chapters of the novel. Immediately I was seized with a desire to attempt such an adaptation myself. I therefore gave Benoît permission to proceed with his French language version, but reserved the rights to any English adaptation for myself.

I started work on my own adaptation of the novel, and it came very easily. I told David Thacker of the project, which I had entitled *Secret Thoughts*, sent him the first draft, and he immediately offered to stage it at the Octagon at the next opportunity, which I accepted gratefully. There were several productions lined up in the queue, and I was writing my novels about Henry James and H.G. Wells in this period, so the Octagon production of *Thinks . . .* did not happen until the spring of 2011. After the usual vain attempts to entice 'star' actors, the play was cast. For Ralph Messenger, David and his Assistant Director Elizabeth Newman favoured Rob Edwards, a versatile actor highly regarded in the profession and well known to a wider audience for his performances with the Royal Shakespeare Company, and in popular television series like *Dr Who* and *Casualty*. When I watched him later in rehearsal I was happy with their choice. Casting the part of Helen proved more difficult. Several excellent actresses whom David knew personally and who had worked with him before were offered the part, but declined apologetically. This was discouraging, but I thought that the main deterrent was probably Bolton itself, a drab and economically depressed town, requiring a change of trains at Manchester for travellers from London, the hub of the acting profession. The prospect of spending ten weeks in Bolton for rehearsals and performances would not appeal to them.

I went up and down between Birmingham and Bolton frequently, staying overnight in the town's principal hotel which belonged to the Holiday Inn chain, a name which struck an incongruous note in this location. The commuting was tiring and time consuming, but I wanted to observe and contribute to the development of the production. It was soon obvious to me that the staff of the theatre were devoted to David, and ready to work their socks off to make the play a success. For example, my script included a scene from the novel in which Messenger and Helen argue while sharing a hot tub at night with snow falling, and the backstage team devoted a lot of time and effort to constructing a very convincing tub which rose out of the stage floor emitting steam, while a simulation of falling snow was projected on to the walls of the auditorium. It always cast a spell on the audience.

Having failed to fill the part of Helen from his usual sources, David selected a local actress called Kate Coogan, who was highly esteemed in Manchester and elsewhere on the northern theatre circuit, and had won regional awards for her performances. She was the mother of several children, the youngest of whom was only a year old, and had been absent from the stage since he was born, but she was now ready and eager to work again. David was impressed when he interviewed her, and I trusted his judgement. But when I met her at the first read-through of the play she seemed very different from *my* Helen, a Cambridge graduate with a PhD on Henry James to her name, brought up in posh Aldeburgh in Suffolk by devoted middle-class parents, who now had her own home in London, for which she pines in her first days at the University of Gloucester. At first Kate's Lancashire accent seemed to me inappropriate to her character in rehearsals, but I was encouraged when she spoke her last speeches in the play with a force and conviction that derived in part from her own natural speech, and I agreed with David that we should not meddle with it.

I went back to Bolton for the dress rehearsal on Wednesday the 11th of May, and stayed there for the preview on Thursday and Press Night on Friday the 13th – an ominous date to the superstitious, as the dress rehearsal seemed to confirm. Kate was in poor form: she had lost all confidence, gabbled her lines, and was sometimes inaudible. I told David afterwards that I thought we were heading for a disaster at the preview, which my agent Leah was coming from London to see. He agreed that Kate had been disappointing, but told me he had booked her for two hours in a closed rehearsal room next morning to get her back on track. He joined me at the Holiday Inn for breakfast and I gave him some notes which he took on board, inviting me to join him and Kate in the rehearsal room. The session was a revelation to me of what a charismatic director can achieve, as he took Kate through her lines and got her to speak them as if she understood and believed every word. Kate was exhausted but happy at the end of the exercise. She knew now what it was to be Helen.

The preview next evening went very well, and Leah was impressed by both the cast and the direction, while warning me that there was little hope of the production transferring to London because the two actors, Kate in particular, were not well known. Later I wished I had persuaded her to come to the Press Night performance instead of the preview (her own choice) because it exceeded all my hopes and expectations. That weekend, back at home, I sent her a jubilant report:

Dear Leah,
The opening on Friday evening went extremely well. Both actors gave their best performances so far. Kate in

161

particular showed a huge advance in confidence and subtlety. Rob exploited the comic possibilities of his role to great effect and elicited a great deal of laughter. The play was rapturously received by an audience who seemed totally absorbed and responded to every nuance. I received many compliments afterwards, and the acting, design, direction and special effects like the tub were widely praised. A member of the Theatre's Board of Management, and till recently its chair, told me it was the best new play she had seen at the Octagon since she became involved with it. A middle-aged actor told me it was the best new play he had seen in years. A couple who had lost count of the plays they had walked out of at the interval said it had restored their faith in theatre as an art form. I couldn't have asked for a better first night. Whether its success with that audience will be reflected in reviews remains to be seen. But my faith in the play has been validated, and I'm sure it will have a future in some form. I hope you'll do your best to persuade some London producers to see the show in its short run.

Best wishes, David

The reviews which appeared in Manchester and its environs were all excellent, and later *Secret Thoughts* received an award for Best New Play of that year in the region. I was particularly encouraged by a reviewer who pointed out that, at a time when few theatrical producers could afford to mount plays with large casts, an entertaining and thought-provoking two-hander like *Secret Thoughts* should attract offers to stage it elsewhere, but to my disappointment that didn't happen. Nothing happened, in fact, until the play was sent to my agent in France, Suzanne Sarquier, who was delighted with it and immediately began to set up a production in Paris. She chose as translator a French playwright, Gérald Sibleyras, who had enjoyed success in Paris with a play set in a retirement home for veterans of World War One. It was adapted and translated into English by Tom Stoppard, entitled *Heroes*, had a good run at Wyndham's Theatre in London, and won the Laurence Olivier Award for Best New Comedy in 2006. I felt sorry that Armand had been passed over as translator, but I could understand Suzanne's thinking: that the association of Gérald's name with my play would attract Parisian theatregoers.

I discovered to my surprise that Gérald was currently living in London with his wife Sylvie, a writer of novels and non-fiction books, and their youngest child, believing that all of them would benefit culturally and linguistically from spending a couple of years in England. Mary and I soon became friends with this lively and sociable couple and enjoyed dinners at their home when we were in London, which we repaid with occasional meals at Groucho's, and an invitation to visit us in Birmingham. Gérald liked the club and I proposed him successfully for membership. Eurostar made it easy for him to get back to Paris when required in the early stages of the production of *Pensées Secrètes*.

Of the several plays I have written in my life, none had so quick a journey to the stage as that one. The pages of this memoir and its predecessors contain plenty of evidence of how difficult, frustrating and time-consuming that process usually is, but this production developed with uncanny ease. In the autumn of 2011, Suzanne arranged a private reading of my play with Isabelle Carré, a very popular actress and something of a star in films as well as plays, as Helen, and Samuel Labarthe, also admired for his work on both stage and screen, as Ralph Messenger. They loved their parts and signed up to act in the play, opening in February of the coming year, directed by Christophe Lidon. When he heard the name, Armand warned me that this man liked to put his stamp on the plays he directed and that I had better be prepared for unconventional effects. *Pensées Secrètes* was to be staged at the Théâtre Montparnasse, opening early in the New Year for a run of several months. It was all arranged and contracted for in a matter of weeks, without any hitches or crises, which seemed almost miraculous to me after my previous theatrical experience.

When I was shown the Théâtre Montparnasse I was enchanted. It was built in the 1880s, '*La Belle Epoque*', and had been beautifully restored and decorated in red and gold. The auditorium had a traditional design with a proscenium stage, circle, gallery and about 700 seats, mostly in the stalls – an ideal space for a two-hander. The contrast with the Bolton Octagon's flexible and well-worn acting space could not have been more striking – as was the difference between the British and French productions of my play. The Montparnasse stage was much smaller than the Octagon's and created an atmosphere of intimacy. Christophe had lived up to his reputation by keeping props to a minimum and requiring the audience to use their imagination. A single desk placed centre stage, for example, served for the offices of both characters, and sometimes they would be speaking to each other by phone while sitting side by side. But what most struck me in the production was the sensuality of the relationship between the pair, especially in the scene when Messenger tries to persuade Helen to share a siesta with him in her bedroom. Samuel gently fingered and stroked Isabelle's hair as he spoke, while she, torn between principle and desire, writhed and struck yoga poses on the floor. In a later scene Ralph dictated his description of their first lovemaking also sitting on the floor, Helen lying with her head pillowed on his thigh, and a look of post-coital satisfaction on her face. The audience responded to the chemistry between the actors, and brought them back for several curtain calls at the end. Isabelle told the audience that I was present, and asked me to stand up in the stalls, so I did, and was applauded.

Myriam, the owner of the theatre, was lurking in the side aisle to take Mary and me under her wing, and immediately asked what I thought of the performance. I replied that it had been marvellous, though actually I thought that the actors were going too fast at the beginning of the play, and should vary the pace more. By now I knew how sensitive actors were about the slightest hint of criticism, and reserved this thought and some others for a note I intended to send Christophe next day. Myriam took us to a comfortable bar and restaurant on the ground floor of the theatre, where we had a drink and something to eat with Leah, who had come over from England for the first night with Stephen Durbridge, senior director of The Agency, and we were joined by the actors in due course. Leah congratulated me warmly on the reception of the play and I thought that, perhaps for the first time, she believed I might become a successful playwright. The enthusiastic reviews of *Pensées Secrètes* in the French press in the days that followed, especially a rave in the Sunday *Figaro*, encouraged that speculation.

When she was back in her London office, Leah was called about some other business by a producer I shall call 'Q', who had enjoyed considerable success in the West End with small-cast comedies that had some cultural or intellectual sophistication. When Leah told him about the first night of *Pensées Secrètes* in Paris he became very excited, and begged her to send him the English text of the play. Although Leah did not like him personally, she recognised that he was someone who could definitely put the play on if he was taken with it, so she sent it to him. He responded enthusiastically, said he wanted to option the play, and invited both of us to lunch at Sheekey's fish restaurant, much patronised by theatre folk, to discuss directors who might be approached to participate. Q was joined at the restaurant by a young man who appeared to be his assistant and companion, and there was some badinage between them before we got down to business. When Q asked if we had any preferences for directors, I suggested Michael Blakemore, and he said, 'I know *exactly* why you think that,' but did not explain why, or commit himself to approaching Michael either then or later.

A few weeks later Leah called me with disappointing news. Q had been to see the play in Paris, and had evidently chosen an evening when the audience was thin and unresponsive. One reason for this was explained to me by Suzanne Sarquier: once again I was unlucky to have a play opening when a presidential election was approaching and most Parisians were glued to their television sets at home in the evenings. Leah sensed that Q was losing confidence in the play, and she discovered that, without consulting us, he had been privately showing the script to other producers and some directors to elicit their opinions without our permission, which was unacceptable professional behaviour. When Leah pressed him about the option he had proposed, he sent a letter backing out. She was disgusted and told me she would not reply, though I could if I wished. I did not so wish, but I was bitterly disappointed. The euphoria of the opening night at the Montparnasse and the enthusiastic reviews in the French press, following the congratulations at the Octagon opening, had made me think that at last I had written a fail-safe play, but evidently I had not. It had taken me a long time to accept that one should never trust first-night audiences or reviews as reliable indices of success.

14

While the dramatisation of *Thinks . . .* was being staged in England and France, the film of *Therapy* was still in development. Progress had been slow, mainly because so many different fingers were in the pie at different times. Although Stephen Evans owned the rights in my screenplay and continued to take an occasional interest in the film, the production was based in the office of Renaissance, in partnership with Trudie Styler's company Xingu. Emails, phone calls and faxes with suggestions for casting and changes in the screenplay pinged back and forth constantly between all the people involved, including myself, Leah, and David Thacker.

The most urgent task to be addressed was casting, especially the part of Tubby, who would be on screen almost throughout the film. These were some of the actors who were approached and sent the screenplay over several years: Ken Stott, Alfred Molina, Bob Hoskins, Tom Wilkinson, Jim Broadbent, Michael Gambon, Mel Smith, Ray Winstone, Warren Clark, and the Australian actor Geoffrey Rush. The latter came into the frame after Leah sent a copy of *Therapy* on her own initiative to Julia Chasman, an

American independent producer she knew who had recently had considerable success with a movie called *Quills* about the Marquis de Sade, in which Rush starred. Julia loved the novel ('*What a wonderfully funny, fully realised character with a story that is by turns hilarious and moving*') and sent it to Rush asking him if he would be interested in the part of Tubby. He wrote me a charming letter in which he said, 'Not many scripts manage to get TV execs, middle-age angst and Kierkegaard on to the same page. Except perhaps vintage Woody.' But he very sensibly pointed out that 'Tubby is inevitably an endomorph. Being of the ecto persuasion I don't offer much in the roly-poly department.' He added that he believed 'the role needed a native Britishness to it', as I did myself; so nothing transpired. From time to time afterwards Julia Chasman came to London and enquired about the progress of our film, but did not make a positive move to get involved. In an email to Leah she shrewdly observed, 'the problem, of course, is that it is already quite overloaded with people and history and commitments in a way that may not be workable'.

None of the actors mentioned above accepted the invitation to play the part of Tubby. David Thacker and I were particularly sorry that Tom Wilkinson turned us down, since we had both collaborated with him in the past and admired his work enormously. But his reasons threw light on the rejections we received from the other actors. David reported to me in an email the gist of a long telephone conversation he had with Tom:

> He doesn't think it will make a feature film . . . he means that there is not enough at stake to drive a film narratively. In his view the central character is reactive, not proactive, and though this may work in a novel, in a film you need a character to be driving the narrative. He found the script – as a read – compelling and a page-turner. He just doesn't think it will make a film. In a nutshell – the stakes are not high enough.

David added, 'This has rather knocked the stuffing out of me, as it will no doubt with you . . . but Tom is an intelligent guy and his views are worth listening to.'

Indeed. I would have qualified Tom's view of the character of Tubby by pointing out that he does constructively drive the last act of the film to a satisfying conclusion by going to Spain to track down Maureen. But I had to acknowledge that Tubby, like most of my British principal male characters, and perhaps myself, is more reactive than proactive. And when he does decide to act – for instance, pursuing various women to avenge himself on his wife for her rejection of him – he often makes a fool of himself. Although reactive male central characters had worked well enough in my novels, I could see that they might not suit the narrative tempo for most British and American feature films.

It wasn't just actors to play Tubby, but also offers to invest in the film that were not forthcoming. As the first years of the new millennium passed, I myself and several people at Renaissance and Xingu were losing hope that a feature film of *Therapy* would ever get made. There came a point when Trudie Styler, who by now had most authority among the key people involved in the project, summoned a meeting to make a final attempt to discuss how it might be rescued. It was held on the top floor of her mansion in St James's. Everyone present had just read the latest version of the screenplay and agreed that it was excellent – so why hadn't it been made? The answer, we concluded, after hearing the opinions of the assembled people, must be the failure to enlist a bankable star, or even a plausible lead actor, for the part of Tubby.

Fred Molina, who many of us thought would fit the part, ruled himself out with rare honesty in a letter to David Thacker: 'This movie needs a greater talent and presence than I can provide . . . I don't have the range to play Tubby.' Others were less explicit about their reasons for declining. Probably at the bottom of most responses was the view of the screenplay that Tom Wilkinson had expressed to David Thacker. We seemed to have come to the end of the road, though nobody explicitly said as much, and the meeting disbanded in a mood of resigned disappointment.

I sent the screenplay to John Archer, my former student at Birmingham University, who was now head of a small film company in Scotland, asking for his opinion. He said it was a clever adaptation of the novel, but I was struck by this comment: 'As a film I found it a lot easier to imagine as a French film rather than a British one. I realise that this may be an odd reaction – it just feels much more likely to be made if it was French, with its range of themes, than to be financed in Britain. I can imagine Bernard Tavernier making it in Lyons.'

There were still occasional encouraging expressions of interest in the project. The most promising came from two talented young men who worked for the Carlton TV company, writing and producing programmes for both BBC and ITV. Carlton had invited them to look for a novel they would like to adapt for television and they chose *Therapy*. They were thinking of casting Timothy Spall as Tubby – an excellent idea, which all of us involved in the process had somehow overlooked. He was physically perfect for the part of Tubby, an endomorph with a homely countenance and a natural manner compatible with the social origins of my character. At this time he was chiefly known for his roles in popular ITV comedy series like *Auf Wiedersehen Pet*, but later in his successful career he would show considerable strength and versatility in the roles he played. I met the two young men, Mark Bussell and Justin Sbresni, and found them sympathetic and intelligent. They made it clear that they would like me to be involved in the development of the script in a consultation role only, which would suit me perfectly. I was now well into my next work of prose fiction, and I didn't want to be distracted by doing any more rewrites of *Therapy*. But eventually I was too doubtful about their ability to produce an adaptation of the novel that would satisfy me, so I pulled out, and the project, like so many, was never realised.

A feature of their plans which had caught my attention was

that they intended to use 'voice over' for Tubby. I recalled that on the very first day I met Stephen Evans, I told him I had been thinking that VO might be an effective way to convey Tubby's unspoken thoughts, which occupy a good deal of textual space in the novel. But Stephen emphatically rejected the idea. As I was keen to encourage his interest in making a film of *Therapy*, I did not mention using voice over again; but when the two guys from Carlton revived it I regretted – too late – that I had not pursued the idea. It suddenly seemed obvious to me that, in the novel, Tubby's character was conveyed mainly by his private thoughts, recorded in his journal, which could have been rendered in voice over in a film, expressing the humour and humanity of his character. I recalled John Archer's remark about my screenplay, '*I found it a lot easier to imagine as a French film rather than a British one.*' French filmmakers frequently use their main characters as voice-over narrators of the story, often a fictional autobiographical story like my novel, and American producers also sometimes favour this method; but for some reason British film producers seldom make use of it and most of them, like Stephen Evans, have a deep prejudice against it.

I had in fact been approached in recent years by several French film producers interested in adapting one or other of my novels as feature films, and had meetings with them in Paris, which sometimes led to an option deal, but no prospect so far of a film actually being made. Meanwhile my publisher Rivages had acquired a new owner, from Switzerland, Jean-François Lamunière. I gathered he had inherited the company rather than purchased it, and owned a vineyard in the Loire region which produced quality wine. He was a man of business with limited knowledge of literature and the book trade and did not involve himself in the editorial side of Rivages, but he was aware that I was the company's bestselling author, and befriended me and Mary. He enjoyed his wealth and a somewhat flamboyant lifestyle, and was very good company. He had a wife and two children whom he installed in a luxuriously modernised flat on the top floor of a restored period house in the

Rue de Tabac, its walls hung with *trompe l'oeil* copies of famous paintings by French Impressionists, and he owned a powerful motorbike on which he arrived, dressed in black leathers, at the premiere of *La Vérité Toute Nue*, while his wife took a cab.

I discovered that Jean-François was a friend of Charles Gassot, a distinguished French film producer, and when I told him about the production-in-progress (or non-progress) of *Therapy* he offered to mention it to Gassot in case he might be interested in a co-production. I thanked him and suggested to the *Therapy* team that they should send Gassot a copy of our script and some information about the film, which had now been budgeted at £4.8 million and was hopefully scheduled for shooting in Copenhagen and Spain in the coming summer. Jean-François, who obviously felt more at home in the movie business than in publishing literary fiction, got busy approaching other possible French co-producers of *Therapy*, including television companies, attracting some interest, but no deals.

15

Early in 2002 I received an invitation from the British Council to go to Argentina in April 2004, to represent the UK at the Buenos Aires Book Fair, a major event of its kind in South America. It would entail a couple of appearances on stage at the Fair, meetings with writers, interviews with journalists, book signings – the usual routine, but also a good deal more, including a chance to see a theatrical adaptation of my novel *Therapy*. An Argentinian writer called Gabriela Izcovich, who was also the director of a small theatre in Buenos Aires, had written to me in 2002 to ask permission to adapt it for dramatic performance. She had adapted some other British and European novels, most recently Hanif Kureishi's *Intimacy*, first published in 1998, a bleak novella about a man who deserts his wife and children to satisfy his desire for a younger woman. Gabriela was briefly in London around the turn of the century, and I arranged to meet her to discuss her ideas for a play of *Therapy*. She was a striking, vivacious woman, probably in her thirties, with typical Latin looks (though her surname indicated some Eastern European element in her lineage), fluent in English and full of enthusiasm for her work in theatre.

That was in the time of Argentina's Great Depression between 1998 and 2002, when the devaluation of the peso led to a run on the banks, which were closed down to prevent the withdrawal of deposits, and most people experienced a drastic decline in their quality of life, which did not improve until 2004. One consequence of this was that commercial theatres in Buenos Aires had gone dark, and been replaced by groups of actors and directors putting on their own shows wherever they could find a suitable space. It was a production of this kind that Gabriela invited me to see when I told her that the British Council was sending me to attend the Book Fair in April 2004. I thought her production of *Therapy* would add something very interesting to my visit and I looked forward to seeing it. Gabriela was delighted, and sent me a sheaf of several of her short stories, written in English, which were brief, witty and accomplished. She was a very versatile lady. I was impressed.

Mary, needless to say, did not for a moment contemplate accompanying me on the long flight to Argentina, and in compensation I promised that after I returned we would have a week's holiday together in Sicily, which neither of us had visited before. The British Council arranged my travel to South America: outward journey on Saturday the 10th of April in business class from Birmingham to Buenos Aires via Frankfurt, with Lufthansa, returning by the same route on Sunday the 18th of April. My trip did not begin auspiciously. On the day before my departure I had symptoms of diarrhoea, which continued intermittently on the journey and during my first two days in Buenos Aires, until I was provided with a miraculous pill obtained by some knowledgeable friend of Gabriela. Next day I was able to eat cautiously from a splendid lunch in the garden of her parents' home, and from then onwards I was fine.

That evening I went to Gaby's theatre and met the cast. I was surprised to discover that they were mostly amateurs with professional day jobs – including a university lecturer, a psychiatrist, an architect, plus some trained actors who had lost their work during the Depression. They rehearsed and performed nearly every evening without pay, for the sheer pleasure of acting. The theatre itself looked as if it had once been a warehouse, which had been gutted to create a high cubic space surrounded by separate banks of seats, a little bit like the Bolton Octagon. On the floor of the central acting space there was a wooden structure of ingenious design which could be detached and reassembled, sometimes while the action was continuing, to provide a number of different objects for sitting and lying on – a bench, a bed or twin beds, a table, chairs, stools and so on, as the plot required.

Everything was done at a fast pace, cutting from scene to scene with minimal explanatory detail. For instance, there is a point in the novel when Tubby's friend Amy, with him in his London flat, says she would like to go somewhere warm for a break, and he suggests Tenerife. In this production, the lighting changes to bright, they turn as if to stare into the distance, and Amy puts on a pair of sunglasses. 'The beach is black!' she exclaims incredulously, and Tubby explains that the Canaries are made of volcanic rock. Immediately we know where they are, and the first note of disappointment, which runs through the whole episode, is struck by the mention of a black beach. The dialogue was all in Spanish, of course, and I had to try and guess what the actors were saying from what I remembered of my own original text and familiarity with the story. I had a feeling that it was a pretty free adaptation, but the audience obviously enjoyed it. Afterwards I went with Gaby and the cast for a celebratory supper at a local restaurant.

Gaby's production was a great success in the Buenos Aires fringe theatre scene, and ran at intervals for months, indeed years. In August 2009 she emailed to me, '*Therapy continues always fine, with a lot of public.*' When I was in Buenos Aires I was pleasantly surprised to find that the novel was also widely read in the Spanish translation, *Terapia*. It was an irresistible title for a novel in Buenos

Aires, whose citizens are famously obsessed with psychoanalysis and which is reputed to have more psychotherapists to the square mile than any other city in the world. Writer's Luck! I had a big crowd and a rapturous reception for my reading of a passage from *Therapy* at the Book Fair, and signed a lot of copies.

In retrospect I think my week in Buenos Aires was possibly the most consistently enjoyable of the many trips of this kind I did for the British Council. There is a long history of friendly relations between our two countries, which had been soured for a period by the Falklands War, but I never sensed any resentment on that subject, so I presumed the people were glad to have seen the back of the junta that provoked it. The British Council team in Buenos Aires was extremely efficient and helpful. When I visited their office by appointment I was pleased to find Paula Varsavsky there to greet me. She is an Argentinian novelist and literary journalist whom I met for the first time in July 1998 in Cambridge at the annual British Council Seminar on Contemporary British Writing. She came to London in advance of my visit to Buenos Aires to interview me for *La Nacion*, the principal Argentinian newspaper. In the course of my stay she helped me buy some of the leather goods which are abundant in Argentina, to take home, and escorted me to several interesting venues in the city, including a tango show one evening. The tango is an Argentinian invention, and a national treasure. It evolved from a combination of European dance music and native South American dance, with a stylised but potent erotic rhythm and movement, and I was glad to see it performed by professionals. The venue resembled a night club, with a circular dance floor and a small band of musicians on a stage above them. There was no participation by the audience after the performance, which was fine by me as I had no idea of how to tango.

I also enjoyed exploring Buenos Aires on my own. The highlight was a visit to the Latin American Art Museum, called MALBA, an elegant modernist building with an amazing collection of art from the subcontinent. I was surprised to note that several portraits of beautiful women, including the most celebrated female artist in this part of the world, the Mexican Frida Kahlo, had fine dark hairs visible on their upper lips. Someone explained to me that Latin American women wore these faint moustaches proudly to demonstrate that they were of pure European stock and had no tincture of blood from the beardless South American Indians in their veins. The Museum generously gave me a number of superbly illustrated books about Latin American art to take home with me. The collection was so heavy that I begged the British Council to mail them to my home, which they kindly did. Later I donated some to the Bournville Art College library.

I went back later to MALBA for an evening event, a dialogue on stage with an interviewer who read out his questions from a script, so it sounded more like an interrogation than a conversation. Afterwards there was a signing session for members of the audience. One middle-aged lady exclaimed to me, 'I love you! I love your books!' as she presented her copies to me. The population of Buenos Aires is mostly of immigrant stock from the Latin countries of Europe – Italy and Spain – and from Jewish communities in Eastern Europe, of which Gaby's family was an example. These origins make them a lively, expressive, demonstrative people. It is customary for Argentinians – at least, those I met in Buenos Aires – to greet friends and relatives of either sex with a kiss on the cheek, or a brush of one cheek on another, and they do it even when introduced to someone for the first time. I found this disconcerting initially, but soon got used to it, and for some time after I returned to England I had to make a conscious effort to suppress the acquired habit of saluting old and new acquaintances in this manner.

My faithful German translator, Renate Orth-Guttmann, lives in the hills outside Frankfurt, and I had arranged to join her and her husband at the airport during the stopover on my way home. I managed to freshen up with a shower in time to meet them at an agreed rendezvous, and over breakfast told them something of my Argentinian experiences, until it was time to take my short flight home to Birmingham. I had not met Renate in the flesh before, and she was as charming as she had seemed to be in her letters. It was a delightful conclusion to a successful and enjoyable trip.

16

While I was revising and polishing the first complete text of *Thinks* . . . in the early 1990s, I was wondering what I would write next. I had no convincing 'idea' for another novel in my head or in my notebook. Then chance brought me one. An independent television company wrote to ask if I would be interested in adapting George Du Maurier's novel *Trilby* as a serial for television. I was certainly interested, and promised to let them know. I was familiar with the title, but had never read the book, so promptly bought the Penguin Classics edition, just published to mark the centenary of the novel's first publication in 1894. I discovered that it concerned a group of young Englishmen learning to be artists under masters in the studios of Paris in the late nineteenth century, and that Trilby was the unusual forename of a young female model of Scottish origin who had befriended them. She was a frequent visitor to their attic studio, where these healthy young Englishmen had erected a trapeze for exercise. All of them liked Trilby, and one was in love with her. There was a subplot attached to her in the character of Svengali, a sinister Jewish musician who discovered that under his hypnosis – but *only* then – Trilby had a wonderful singing voice.

Another feature of her character is that she occasionally posed in the nude, which French artists referred to as *le tout ensemble* and she called 'the altogether', which made her a problematic yet titillating heroine for the prudish Victorian reading public.

As a novel *Trilby* was a kind of sanitised, Anglicised and updated version of Henri Murger's enormously popular *Scènes de la Viede Bohème*, first published in 1851, a collection of stories about the aspiring artists of Paris in the early nineteenth century and the young working women who had transient sexual liaisons with them. That book introduced the adjective 'Bohemian' into colloquial English, denoting a liberated and unconventional lifestyle especially associated with artists. I thought the early chapters of *Trilby* had a period authenticity and charm, but as a novel it was poorly constructed, melodramatic and cloyingly sentimental. The historian and psychoanalyst Daniel Pick mentioned in his introduction that Professor Frank Kermode had told him it was the worst novel he had ever read. That seemed to me a rather harsh judgement, but I could see no way to make its story credible or interesting to a modern television audience, and replied to the TV people accordingly.

But two facts in Pick's introduction to the Penguin edition made a strong impression on me. The first was that Henry James had been closely involved in the genesis of *Trilby*. He was a good friend of Du Maurier, who was born of an English mother but brought up in France, and adopted painting as a profession until he lost the sight of one eye. He then switched to the medium of black on white, producing drawings and etchings which were a popular form of illustration in British novels and journals. In due course he emigrated to England and became famous for his cartoons in *Punch*, which Henry James had admired since his youth in America. Their friendship began when James requested that Du Maurier should illustrate the first edition of his novel *Washington Square*, and after James moved from a long residence in Paris to London in 1876, the two men became close friends. They often took walks together in the streets and squares of London and on Hampstead Heath, which was very accessible from Du Maurier's house in Hampstead village where he lived with his wife and five children. On one of these strolls James was complaining that he couldn't think of a plot for his next novel, and Du Maurier, who had modest but genuine aspirations to write fiction himself, offered him the story of Trilby and Svengali which he had been privately nursing for years without doing anything with it. James thanked him, but declined on the grounds that there was too much about music in the story for him to handle. He was tone deaf, and music was the one art in which he took no interest.

The other fact in Pick's introduction which made me sit up was that *Trilby* was believed to be the best selling novel in English published in the nineteenth century. Its sales were huge in America as well as Britain, and made Du Maurier a rich man. It struck me that this must have been an ironic twist in their friendship, given James' disappointment with the meagre income he earned from his own novels. I couldn't help wondering if he later regretted turning down Du Maurier's offer of the story of Trilby and Svengali. In fact, they remained good friends and Du Maurier's family residence in Hampstead continued to be a second home to HJ. I began to think that perhaps I did have a new idea for a novel – one about this relationship. I was aware that there had been several novels about the real lives of authors published in recent years. Beryl Bainbridge's *Queenie* (2001), about the private life of Dr Samuel Johnson, was the first example of this trend to catch my attention, and henceforth it proved an increasingly attractive formula for what the book trade calls 'literary fiction'.

I was also aware that Henry James did not have a large readership, apart from other writers and academics, and was regarded as a difficult and prolix novelist by many people who sampled his work. But it seemed to me that by describing his warm relationship with the more engaging paterfamilias character of Du Maurier, it would be possible to overcome the prejudice against him. I needed to know more about both men for this purpose, so I read Leon Edel's definitive biography of James from cover to cover for the first time, and also an excellent and lavishly illustrated biography of George Du Maurier by Leonée Ormond, published in 1969. This enjoyable exercise convinced me that the contrast between the characters and fortunes of these two writer-friends, and the interweaving of their respective lives were full of narrative possibilities. James was to be the main character of the novel I envisaged, but Du Maurier's part of the story would provide an interesting foil to James'. I had observed that the disastrous first night performance in London of James' play *Guy Domville* in January 1895, when he was booed on stage by the gallery, having been unwisely encouraged to take a bow, happened at about the same time that Du Maurier was enjoying enormous success with his novel *Trilby*, which was soon turned into a successful play. The more research I did, the more connections, symmetries, ironies and reversals I discovered in their lives.

I wrote my novel with a serene confidence in its merit. The research was sheer pleasure and took me, usually with Mary, to interesting places – from Whitby on the coast of north-east England, where James occasionally joined the Du Maurier family for holidays, to Venice, where the American novelist Constance Fenimore Woolson, who was James' friend and companion in England for many years, offered him a love he could not accept and took her own life. I had a special affection for her as a character because she was partially deaf, and obliged to use an ear trumpet to converse with James. When I showed the completed novel to my publishers, they were more enthusiastic than I had dared to hope, quickly accepted the book, and against my expectation, offered an advance as substantial as the previous one for *Thinks* ... My American publishers were equally impressed. I called this novel *Author, Author*, because the two main characters were both writers, and because in England it was, and perhaps still is, the traditional summons from the audience at the end of a new play for the playwright to take his bow. I left Henry James in that posture in the last words of the book.

Later I wrote of it: 'I have never produced a novel I enjoyed writing more, or one I enjoyed publishing less.' The reason for the latter clause was a phone call I received in September 2003 from Jonny Pegg, who had been Mike Shaw's assistant at Curtis Brown until his recent retirement, and was currently acting as my agent. He told me about a very satisfactory offer from my American publishers for *Author, Author*, and then his voice faltered as he reported something that was 'not very nice'. It was that he had sent the text of *Author, Author* to my Polish publisher, who had declined it because they had just contracted to publish a novel about Henry James entitled *The Master* by Colm Tóibín, which was currently being printed in England by Picador for publication in 2004, when *Author, Author* was also scheduled to be published.

I knew immediately that this was very bad news for me. When two books on the same subject by writers of similar status are published in the same year, the first one to appear will usually cream off most of the reader interest, high-profile reviews, prize nominations, and sales. This is especially likely if the subject of both books is one, such as the life of Henry James, that will attract a limited audience. And so it proved, when *Author, Author* was eventually published. To add to my discomfiture, the coincidence was rendered almost farcical by the circumstance that an extraordinary number of other novels about Henry James were being written by other authors and published over the same period. One of them, by the South African writer Michiel Heyns was declined by a publisher who wrote regretfully to him, 'I am so sorry but timing is all – and there has been a spate of fiction based on the life of Henry James published here. I don't know how such coincidences happen.'

I had some theories about that, and I aired them, relieving my frustration and disappointment at being scooped by Colm Tóibín, by writing a long account of the whole experience. It subsequently formed the first part of a new book, *The Year of Henry James or, Timing Is All: the Story of a Novel. With other essays on the genesis, composition and reception of literary fiction*. It was published in 2006 by Harvill Secker, as the imprint was now called following a merger. To readers who are interested in the details of this episode in my life and the light it throws on the writing and publishing of prose fiction, I would recommend that they read the first part of that book.

My publishers in Britain, France and America all made a big effort to promote *Author, Author*, conscious that it was not the kind of novel that my regular readers expected. I did the usual round of literary festivals in the UK, beginning with the Rye Festival, where I had once again agreed to deliver the annual Henry James lecture. But the Festival director suggested instead a dramatised reading of a section of the novel, pointing out that there were several gifted actors resident in and around Rye. With this encouragement I wrote a script for several voices about the first night of *Guy Domville*, which was performed by some of those actors, including my old friend Danny Moynihan, who lived in nearby Hastings. It was presented in the Rye Methodist Chapel, with myself in the pulpit as Narrator, and went down well with the congregation.

When the novel was published later by Rivages, they plastered the windows of Parisian bookshops with huge posters advertising it, and brought Mary and me to France to do signings and interviews. I was invited to take part in the Toulouse Arts Festival, a major cultural event, and Rivages had my dramatised reading translated so that it could be presented there. It was performed by accomplished professional actors, but it did not go down well with the large audience, who were hoping to be amused. As they left the auditorium an elderly lady in the line caught my eye because she was staring at me. As she passed my seat she paused and shook her head reproachfully. 'How *could* you?' she said, in English, and moved on before I could reply.

I was hoping for a more positive reception in America, but I was disappointed by the early reviews of *Author, Author* there, which mostly compared it unfavourably to *The Master*. Colm Tóibín was a new voice in English language fiction and he was impressing readers in the USA as well as the UK. Americans like to back winners and have little time for losers, whether they are sportsmen or writers. The journal most sympathetic to me was *Entertainment Weekly* which said: 'Meet the year's unluckiest good novelist. Lodge had the bright idea to fictionalize the life of Henry James ... Then Colm Tóibín beat him to the finish line.' The later, more considered reviews in newspapers and magazines from all over the States, however, yielded many complimentary quotes for the paperback edition when it was published though nothing as gratifying as a handwritten note from Harold Pinter which I received on the 11th December 2004:

Dear David Lodge,
    I've had such a wonderful time reading *Author, Author*. It's such a rich and deeply impressive piece of work. I thank you for it.

Sincerely, Harold Pinter.

I had accepted an invitation to speak at that year's Chicago Humanities Festival and my editor at Viking, Paul Slovak, had arranged a programme of events to promote *Author, Author* afterwards in New York, Boston and Washington. The first of these was a 'reading' at the 'Y' on 92nd Street, a cultural community centre which is the most favoured venue for literary events in the city, on the 1st of November. The next day happened to be the eve of a presidential election, for which the contenders were the incumbent Republican President, George W. Bush, and the Democrat Senator, John Kerry, so I arrived in Boston at a very interesting moment. The voters of Boston and the state of Massachusetts were predominantly Democrat supporters and were sure to back Kerry, but the fate of the rest of the country was in the balance.

The evening of the election I went to a party at the home of my friend, Susan Suleiman, for her friends and colleagues at

Harvard. After an excellent buffet, we sat round the TV to watch the results coming in from all over the States. The group split up around midnight when it was clear that the result would depend on the vote in Ohio which would not be announced until the following morning. When it came, it was a narrow victory for Bush, tainted by some suspicion about the machinery of the voting procedure in Florida. I was due to be interviewed on radio early that morning, and to give a reading later at the Harvard Bookstore. My driver escort to the studio told me that she and her husband were thinking of emigrating, and her best friend was in tears, so stricken by the result that she was unable to get out of bed. My driver warned me that there might not be much of an audience in the Bookstore that morning, but it was well filled when I arrived. For my reading from *Author, Author* I chose a passage which I had not used before, taken from the very end of the chapter about the disastrous first night of *Guy Domville*, as Henry James walks home afterwards from the theatre in Haymarket to his flat in Kensington, alone with his thoughts. It begins: '*So it was over. He had come to the dead end of the road. The rock wall at the end of the tunnel. Failure.*' It seemed to strike a chord with my audience.

Friends and new acquaintances in America often asked me what I thought of *The Master*, and were always surprised when I replied that I hadn't read it. I abstained from doing so for a year or more to avoid brooding too much on my bad luck, and conversations which would inevitably involve comparative value judgements about which I could not pretend to be unbiased. I wrote in *The Year of Henry James*: 'Only time will tell whether *The Master* is a better book than *Author, Author*, or vice versa, or whether they are equally admirable in different ways, or equally negligible.' By then I had already formed my private opinion on the matter.

In the years that followed, the 'biographical novel' flourished as a genre, and became a subject for academic books, courses and conferences. I decided to write another one myself, this time about H.G. Wells. It was prompted by an invitation to write the introduction to a new Penguin Classics edition of his novel *Kipps*, first published in 1905. It was one of his humorous, Dickensian novels, and one of the most popular, about a humble draper's assistant who unexpectedly inherits a large fortune and struggles to live up to it socially. I had published essays about Wells' fiction before, but in preparation for my Introduction I read his own *Experiment in Autobiography*, and other sources of biographical information.

The more I read, the more fascinating and extraordinary his life and character appeared. His tireless energy for writing books and seducing women, the scrapes and scandals in which he was involved, and his controversial role in the activities of the left-wing Fabian Society, soon convinced me that he would be a fascinating subject for a biographical novel. When I told Jonny Geller (who was now my permanent agent at Curtis Brown, as well as a senior executive of the company) of this idea he was supportive, but the more I thought about it the less feasible it seemed to make a novel-shaped narrative out of the mountain of facts I had accumulated about Wells, and I actually wrote to Jonny to say that I was dropping the idea. He did not question my decision – but I did so myself over the following weekend, and after much cogitation arrived at a plan for the novel. I would organise the story chronologically in five sections, each of which foregrounded one of five especially important women in Wells' life: his cousin Isabel, who became his first wife in 1891, but could not satisfy his sexual appetite, leading to a divorce; his student Amy Catherine Robbins, whom he married in 1894, renaming her 'Jane', who helped him to build his prosperous career as a writer, managed his household and tolerated his infidelities until she died in 1927; Amber Reeves, the daughter of a New Zealand diplomat based in London, a brilliant and beautiful teenager of radical views who had a crush on Wells and an affair with him when she was an undergraduate at Cambridge; Elizabeth von Arnim, an Australian writer unhappily married to a German count, who became a popular novelist in England and Wells' mistress for several years with Jane's approval; and finally Rebecca West, the militant feminist and gifted writer who bore Wells a son (the writer Anthony West) and was the most important woman in Wells' life (though by no means the only one) during its last phase.

Wells was no Adonis; he was short in stature and corpulent in midlife, but he exerted an apparently irresistible erotic power over the opposite sex. One of his biographers whose work I consulted claimed that many women who had sexual relations with him remarked that he was exceptionally well endowed, as well as skilled in the art of seduction. I decided to call this novel *A Man of Parts*. My editor Geoff Mulligan often commented on the appropriateness of this title as we worked on the book together.

The idea of writing a biographical novel about Wells of the same kind and on the same scale as *Author, Author* was particularly attractive to me because Henry James and Herbert Wells, though utterly different in their backgrounds, temperaments and literary aims, were friends, read each other's books and corresponded frequently until late in James' life when Wells wrote a satirical novel about the contemporary literary world in which he mocked the mannered prose style of James' later work, and the older man terminated the relationship in a calm but crushing letter. The abundance and availability of letters to and from the historical persons who figured in these novels was another factor which helped me to write them; and the fact that the action of *Author, Author* takes place partly at the time of the First World War, and *A Man of Parts* at the time of World War Two, was another link between them. They matched each other like two bookends.

17

I was eighty on the 28th of January, 2015. I did not have a party to celebrate the event – just a Sunday lunch for the family, including children and grandchildren, in a private room at a restaurant in Birmingham's City Centre. I was grateful to have reached this point in life with mind and body in fairly good condition, but I did not regard it as a reason for celebration. The eighties are not usually a fertile time of life for writers, especially novelists, unless they happen to have started writing this kind of literature relatively late, and have a hoard of unexploited experience to draw on for composing narrative fiction. Novelists who begin writing and publishing early in life and continue to produce a new novel at regular intervals into late middle age, tend to fall silent at some point in their ninth decade, if they live that long.

Writing a novel is, I believe, the most demanding literary task of all, except perhaps the long narrative poem in stanzaic form, which is rarely attempted these days. Novels of any value usually take a long time to write, unless they are novellas, and may require a lot of preliminary research before composition begins. The writer must live with a novel in progress for months, often a year or more, constantly revising and rewriting, and always thinking of new ways to improve it. It is an obsessive occupation, and mentally taxing. It is one's brain that writes the novel, and brains function less efficiently in old age. The faculty of memory, both long-term and short-term, becomes weaker, and so does the capacity to make illuminating connections between diverse things, concepts and experiences. Finding an original 'idea' for a new novel becomes more and more difficult.

I had made many notes well before my eightieth birthday about possible subjects and stories for another novel, but without feeling sufficiently confident about any of them to start writing. But one morning, when I was shaving in my bathroom, looking into the mirror above the sink and irritated by the buzzing of the electric shaver amplified by my expensive hearing aids, though reluctant to take them out of my ears in case one of them got wet or fell on to the floor or mysteriously went missing, as sometimes happened, I recalled a sentence I had read or overheard, though I could not remember the context. It was: '*Blindness is tragic, but deafness is comic.*' I spoke the sentence aloud to the face in the mirror. It seemed very true to me, confirmed by many literary examples, from *Oedipus Rex* to the farcical mishearing of words by deaf characters in comedies. It occurred to me that this antithesis might inspire a novel.[1]

I began by conceiving a central character called Desmond Bates, Professor of Linguistics at a provincial university in the north-east Midlands, who has recently been persuaded by the administration to take early retirement, thus saving money for the university, and is rather bored by it, while his wife Winifred, formerly a mature student whom he tutored, leads an active and fulfilling life running a soft furnishings business. Desmond suffers from the most common kind of hearing loss in later life, 'high-frequency deafness', caused by the deterioration of the hair cells in the inner ear, which makes it

[1] I tried googling its source while writing this, but the only one offered was my own novel, so perhaps I created it.

difficult to hear the consonants in speech distinctly – such as the terminal phonemes of the words 'deaf' and 'death', for example. Early on in the project I decided on *Deaf Sentence* as the title of this novel. Desmond has been sentenced to deaf.

The catalyst which changes the humdrum tenor of his life in retirement is the arrival at the university of an American postgraduate student, Alex Loom, who has read and admired his published work and persuades him to advise her about her PhD thesis in progress, entitled *A Stylistic Analysis of Suicide Notes*. I had encountered that startling title several years before, as a footnote reference in a book about verbal style. The contrast between the cool academic term, 'stylistic analysis', and the emotively loaded word 'suicide' to which it was applied, caused the phrase to be stored in my memory, though I had never made any mention of it in my writing to date. Now its time had come. What kind of person would choose such a morbid thesis subject, I wondered, and why? My concept of the character of Alex was that she was attractive, friendly, amusing – but also exploitative and unpredictable, and that she would use her extravert personality to infiltrate Desmond's professional and domestic life, stimulating but also sometimes embarrassing and compromising him. The subject she chose for her PhD thesis would serve as a clue to her character and her background, striking a note of danger.

I was pleased with the way *Deaf Sentence* developed, and with its reception when it was published in 2008. There was a lot of interest from the deaf community, though I don't think the book pleased many of its members when they read it, because they do not regard profound deafness as a disabling affliction, but a condition they live with happily and successfully. However, I received a lot of letters from readers who were partially deaf themselves or had partners and other relatives who were, thanking me for encouraging some of those who had stubbornly resisted the idea of wearing hearing aids to do so, and for rendering accurately, but also humorously, the stress that deafness causes in families. One in seven of the UK population suffers significant hearing loss.

The novel gathered excellent reviews in both Britain and the USA, and later in France in the translation by Maurice Couturier, who came up with a brilliant title, *La Vie en Sourdine* (*Life in Mute*) with its piquant echo of the Edith Piaf song, 'La Vie en Rose'. There was some interest in the film and television rights, and an adaptation was actually commissioned by the BBC with my agreement and submitted to me. But I did not feel able to give it my blessing, nor did I offer to attempt a screenplay myself, as I was fully occupied with writing *A Man of Parts* at that time.

To write *Deaf Sentence* I drew on my own experience, as novelists usually do; but I went further in this direction than before in basing the character of Desmond's father, Harry Bates, very closely on my own father, Bill Lodge, whose career as a musician and singer and occasional actor in nonspeaking parts on television I described in previous memoirs. He had been living alone, following my mother's death in 1981, in the semi-detached house in south-east London to which he and Mum had brought me as a year-old infant. I would not have described his character in such detail if he had still been alive to read it. In the last decade of the century he was in his late nineties, showing distinct signs of encroaching dementia, and it was a blessing that he died before the condition became seriously distressing. I tried to describe him as he was then, truthfully and humorously, but with love.

Deaf Sentence is very much a novel about families, the diverse characters of different generations they contain, and the interaction between them. Desmond's dad brings some fun to the Boxing Day party given by Des and Winifred to their cultured friends by over-indulging in the wine, as does Desmond himself, having run out of batteries for his hearing aids, and totally dominating conversations with his guests in monologues, to disguise the fact that he can't hear or respond to them. As this novel approached its end, it became more and more autobiographical, as if the memoirs I had been writing lately were exerting an influence on it. I sent Desmond on a journey I made to a British Council event in Cracow, Poland, in November 1999, and he takes the opportunity to visit nearby Auschwitz and Birkenau, as I did myself. Recovering from that daunting experience in my Cracow hotel in the evening, I received a cheering message from Birmingham that I had a new granddaughter, called Fiona, born that day to my son Stephen and his wife Una, and that went into the novel too.

I intuited that some of my Jewish literary friends had reservations about the Auschwitz episode when they read the novel, which did not surprise or offend me. Jewish people understandably regard the history of the Holocaust as a part of their heritage which cannot be fully understood or assimilated by gentiles, especially those like me who have no familial connections with the victims. I completely understand their point of view. But the exposure of the horrors of the Belsen concentration camp when it was liberated in 1945 and the images that were shown in newspapers and newsreels then, made a powerful impact on me at the age of ten, as I described in my novel *Out of the Shelter*, and were a gruesome prelude to later and more horrific revelations about camps like Auschwitz, which were specifically designed to exterminate the Jewish race, and instilled in me a lasting interest in the history of the Holocaust. I do not regret writing the chapter in *Deaf Sentence* which describes Desmond standing alone and meditative in Birkenau beside the memorial to the victims of Auschwitz on a dark and freezing night; and later some Jewish correspondents wrote appreciative letters to me about it.[2]

[2] Not far from the original Auschwitz, Birkenau is a large, flat area where the Nazis built a railway station to receive the Jews expelled from Germany and countries it occupied, and selected those to be marched directly to the gas chambers prepared for them.

18

In May 2014 I received an invitation to take part in an International Literary Festival to be held in Iaşi, the second city of Romania, in the north-eastern side of the country, at the end of September. I was hesitant to commit myself to any more of such events, since my impaired hearing made them something of a strain in public speaking, on-stage interviews and casual conversation. This invitation came from the chief organiser of the Festival, Lucian Dan Teodorovici, a charming man who revealed that he was a novelist too, and that one of his books had been translated and published in England. I was astonished when he told me the Festival would pay me a fee of 5000 euros for my participation, and fly me business class between London and Bucharest. He extended the invitation to include Mary, but she was not inclined to fly to Romania, so I went on my own.

I knew that my books were remarkably popular in Romania. Every one of my novels to date had been translated and published there by my publisher, Polirom, except the first one (*The Picturegoers*), an immature work which I do not usually agree to circulate in translation. I was told that the Penguin 'Campus Trilogy' (*Changing Places, Small World* and *Nice Work* bound together in a single paperback book) was sold in a special edition on newsstands as well as bookshops in Bucharest. I also had a personal academic link with the country. Professor Lidia Vianu at Bucharest University, officially retired, but still extremely active in teaching, supervising and publishing work about English literature, had asked me if I would address one of her classes via a television satellite link. Impressed by her knowledge and enthusiasm, I agreed. This led to regular correspondence and occasional collaboration between us. She was devoted to my fiction and criticism, and with my willing consent published anthologies of extracts from my books of both kinds, designed for Romanian students in a dual-language format.

The University of Iaşi (the place name is pronounced 'Yash') heard of my forthcoming participation in the Literary Festival, and made an attempt to get involved – even to take it over, offering to fly me and Mary to Romania in business class and to accommodate us in a University-owned villa specially reserved for VIP visitors. I accepted the offer of an honorary doctorate but explained that my travel and accommodation had already been arranged by the Festival, and I was in Iaşi for only five days. The accommodation was a grand hotel designed and built by the architect of the Eiffel Tower. My room was vast, but sparsely furnished, with no suitable surface on which to write notes about my journey, and inadequate curtains on an east-facing window which woke me early with the rising sun in the mornings.

The history of Romania is full of conflict, violence and suffering, but I had arrived at a time of relative calm and prosperity. The expulsion and execution of the tyrannical Communist head of state, Nicolae Ceauşescu, in 1989, the year the Berlin Wall was breached and the states of Eastern Europe began to rebel against Soviet control, had brought freedom to the country, and most of the people on the streets seemed cheerful and contented. Having read Patrick McGuiness's brilliant and gripping novel about the end of Ceauşescu's oppressive regime, *The Last Hundred Days*, on my flight to Bucharest, I understood why.

The citizens of Iași are a religious people, roughly 50 per cent Greek Orthodox and 25 per cent Roman Catholic, and they were obviously glad to be free to practice their Christian faith openly. On my first morning I strolled with Codrin down the long avenue that connected my hotel to the Palace of Culture where the Festival events would take place. He was to be my interlocutor at the opening session of the Festival that evening, knew my work very well and spoke perfect English. On the way we went into the Greek Orthodox cathedral where a mass was in progress, chanted from behind a screen while the congregation milled about in the nave in the usual uninhibited GO way, utterly different from a RC mass. After lunch in a rather chilly marquee outside the Palace of Culture I went back to the hotel to rest. Later I was driven to the National Theatre of Iași to test the sound system and translation facilities for my appearance that evening, which was a conversation with Codrin about my work and a short reading. The theatre had a classic horseshoe shape with three levels, beautifully furnished and decorated. Gradually the seats were occupied, until it was a full house, a spectacle which I always found stimulating when I was about to perform. But the start of the event was delayed by a series of speeches by various dignitaries celebrating the occasion, a ritual familiar to me from similar occasions in European venues.

Meanwhile I had been impressed by the efficiency of the technicians and their equipment. Both the writers who were to speak and members of the audience were provided with in-the-ear receivers like hearing aids which provided everyone with simultaneous translation in either English or Romanian as they chose – a system I had never experienced before. The stage management was not so good: the chairs for me and Codrin had been placed right at the back of the stage, so I asked the stagehands to bring them to the front to create some connection with the audience. Then they took away the lectern which I had requested for my reading, and had sheepishly to bring it back to the amusement of the house. Our conversation went well, though some guests complained to me afterwards that Codrin said too much, showing off his knowledge of my work – which was true, so I was glad I had a reading ready. I read the first page or two of *Deaf Sentence* which has some laughs in it, and it was clear from the audience's reaction that a large proportion of them understood spoken English very well. Always when I am on the Continent I am conscious of my linguistic limitations, and impressed by the fact that almost every native of any country knows some English, and many are fluent. Why are we Brits generally so hopeless in this respect? Mainly of course because English is the lingua franca of the modern world, and we lazily rely on that – at least I do.

My reading went well and several members of the audience later told me I was a better speaker of my text in English than the professional actor who read the passages in Romanian. I was also told that our conversation had been recorded and would be aired on Romanian TV, and later that it could be viewed on YouTube. I could hardly believe that at the time, but forgot about it until I was writing this chapter, and my granddaughter Fiona, who is completely at ease with the internet, quickly traced it for me. I have just watched it for a while. It is not very easy to follow the dialogue because the English and Romanian versions of the three-cornered conversation overlap and interfere with each other, but the audience listened attentively and applauded warmly at the end of the session.

Afterwards many people came up to me to have their copies of my books signed, but there was no formal signing session. We went off to the Radisson Hotel where there was a reception with finger food and excellent wine. I amused the group I was with by telling them about the size of my hotel room and its exiguous curtains, at which the Head of Local Government looked concerned. 'That is not right,' he said. 'I will see to it.' I begged him not to bother, but he shook his head. 'You will find it fixed when you return to your room,' a lady in the group said to me. And she was right.

The next day was mainly taken up with interviews with press, radio and TV journalists, co-ordinated by my Romanian literary agents, two lively and efficient ladies, Simone and Andrea. Simone, jolly and motherly, used to work for my publishers, Polirom, before she founded her agency with the younger Andrea as partner. They followed me around to my various engagements in the course of the week and were extremely helpful. That evening I went back to the National Theatre to hear the main speaker, the Mexican film writer and director Guillermo Arriaga, whose latest film, *Babel*, had caused quite a stir in England. He spoke in fluent idiomatic English in a humorous style, and attracted a full house too. According to Patrick McGuinness, Romanians were historically devoted to film, and before World War Two, Bucharest had more cinemas per head than any other capital in Europe.

The next day, and the last but one of my visit, was mainly spent at the University, where I was to be awarded the honorary D.Litt. I had received a few such honours before in my career, and politely declined several others. I did not enjoy the ritual of dressing up in robes, processing through the assembled audience, mounting the stage and doffing one's tassled mortar board to the senior academics present, never quite sure about the protocol. However the University of Iași put on a good show for me. There was music and a male choir who sang religious and patriotic songs. A professor called Veronica (I didn't catch her surname) read the Laudatum, a speech praising my achievements which was printed and bound in a small booklet and given to me. Then I gave a prepared speech myself. I spoke about the difference between Anglo-American and Continental European critical approaches to English literature, and the rise of creative writing as a popular subject in British universities. I gathered from conversation in the lunch break that the Iași staff did not regard it as a suitable subject for tertiary education, which did not surprise me. The ethos of the University was traditional scholarship, leavened by some recent developments in critical theory.

Before lunch there was a reception with sparkling white wine, in the course of which I was ambushed by a professor with a former graduate of the University in tow, a mature blonde lady whose PhD thesis on my work, written some years ago, he had supervised. She presented me with the thesis in two heavy volumes, which Simone kindly took charge of, entitled *David Lodge: Novel Wor(l)ds and Mediated Communication*, which seemed to be about the reception of my work, but was obviously influenced by the rise of deconstructionist theory, as the contrived pun in the title indicated. She also presented me with other gifts: a white dress shirt with the insignia of the University on the points of the collar, cufflinks to match, a UI tie and a heavy book about the University and its history. There followed a long bibulous lunch at one of the city's best restaurants, which I slept off in the afternoon back at the Grand Hotel.

That evening I returned to the National Theatre for the climactic event of the Festival, which was an appearance by the writer Herta Müller, who had been awarded the Nobel Prize for Literature in 2009 and was something of a heroine to the Romanian public. Ethnically she belonged to a small German-speaking minority, from a part of the old Austro-Hungarian Empire embedded within modern-day Romania, a vulnerable position to occupy in that period of European history. She wrote about her people and their suffering – notably the deportation of many to the Russian Gulags for forced labour, during the Soviet occupation of Romania after the end of World War Two. Her work led to her harassment and persecution by Ceauşescu's government until it was overthrown. She received rapturous applause when she walked on to the stage of the National Theatre, a small, slim woman in a simple black dress. She was in conversation with a psychiatrist who had worked in that capacity throughout the Ceauşescu regime, but admitted that he had compromised with it to some extent in order to continue in his vocation. He was a shrewd, civilised man whose calm manner contrasted with Müller's volatile, emotional temperament, swinging between hilarious and sombre memories of living in a police state, which she kept returning to, and from which one felt she would never be free.

On my last day I had arranged to be shown around the city and environs by Professor Veronica and Codrin, and we were joined by his wife and a couple of other academics. We visited a Greek Orthodox fortified monastery of the sixteenth and seventeenth centuries, and then had a long and delicious lunch in a restaurant serving traditional Romanian food such as stuffed cabbage, accompanied by excellent wine. After lunch the ladies escorted me to a jewellery shop in a shopping mall where I bought a pretty earring and necklace set of silver and agate as a gift for Mary. Then I went back to the hotel to rest before my departure. I had discovered before I left England that there was a direct flight from Iași to Birmingham which departed near midnight, and was used primarily by Romanians looking for work in England, mostly in agriculture. I decided to forgo the comfort of business class for the return leg to London from Bucharest, and booked for the direct flight to Birmingham airport, which would be only a half-hour taxi ride distant from home and a full English breakfast. I returned with pleasant memories of my brief sojourn in Iași and its hospitable Literary Festival. I never did work out why I am so popular in Romania – why all my novels are translated there, and none of them in neighbouring Hungary, for instance. But my self-esteem certainly got a boost while I was there, and it encouraged me to go on writing as I approached my eightieth year and ninth decade.

19

Deaf Sentence (2008), as I write this on New Year's Day 2021, was the last wholly fictional novel with an invented story which I wrote and published, and it was a successful one. The long column of review quotes inside the cover of the Penguin edition of 2009 could not have been more gratifying to the author. '*Enjoyable, thought-provoking,*' ... '*Lodge at the top of his game,*' ... '*sophisticated, beautifully layered . . . speaks to the intellect as well as the senses,*' ... '*As moving as it is entertaining.*' And so on. The book was also well received in translation in France and other European countries, in the USA and other continents. I had ideas for more novels briefly sketched in my notebook, but I was not sufficiently convinced to make a start on any one of them. I wondered if in fact I had another novel in me. I continue to wonder, reluctant to give up hope.

In April 2009 Margaret Drabble published a book called *The Pattern in the Carpet: A Personal History with Jigsaws.* She had been fascinated by jigsaws since childhood. Collecting and studying them in adulthood offered her some relief from the stress of writing literary novels. She says in a remarkable passage:

The hours of freedom from words are a relief to me, though paradoxically I then seem to feel the need of words to try and analyse the nature of this freedom. That's because writing is an illness. A chronic, incurable illness. I caught it by default when I was twenty-one, and I often wish I hadn't. It seemed to start off as therapy, but it became the illness it set out to cure ... Writing is a protection, a cure, an affliction. It makes you ill and it offers to cure you. Writers need a rest from words, words, words.

To aspiring novelists struggling to get their work published this statement will seem almost blasphemous. Teachers and manuals of creative writing often advise their pupils to write something – *anything*, rather than nothing – every day. To writers who build careers by a steady production of books which appeal to a certain readership and thus secure their place in the collective cultural consciousness, the drain on a writer's energy and stamina will sometimes feel like a kind of illness, as it did evidently to Margaret Drabble.

The really interesting aspect of this subject is the enormous number of people today who long to be novelists. Creative Writing is one of the most popular options in the curricula of university degree courses, and extra-mural courses thrive. The internet provides an outlet for self-publishing of new fiction, occasionally throwing up work of genuine interest and originality. For writers of my generation contemporary literary fiction was in adolescence a portal to adulthood, and especially to the depiction of adult sexual behaviour – which was not then as widely and frankly represented and discussed as it is today. This led me to write a scene depicting sexual intercourse between two young minor characters in *The Picturegoers*, when I myself was still a virgin. It was a risky undertaking, but no reader commented adversely on it.

*

I think I have had a successful career as a writer, without achieving the dizzy heights of fame. All my novels are still in print and most circulate in various foreign translations and in other formats, such as e-books. I earned quite a lot of money from some of them, directly or indirectly, and it gave me great satisfaction to enhance the lives of my family and myself from this source of income. I have not said much about my plays in this respect, but occasionally they yielded significant royalties. My readers may be wondering if this degree of success did not dispel the depression and anxiety which I mentioned at the beginning of this book. It has certainly helped to overcome depression, but I inherited a susceptibility to anxiety from genetic sources in my family background, and I doubt if I shall ever be free from it. However I am well aware that I have had a fortunate career as an author, and am duly grateful to those who have nourished it in various ways.

Writing has been the staple occupation of my life. In 2014 I published a book of short biographical essays about the lives of nine writers and a famous personage who wasn't a writer, but much written about. The book was called *Lives in Writing* and Harvill Secker gave it a bright yellow jacket, with the author's name and the title arranged vertically in brown, and images of pens and pencils of various kinds placed between them.

It was my friend and fellow writer Bernard Bergonzi who was the first to point out to me that when the list is read vertically the word 'LIVES' acquires two possible meanings: as the plural of the noun 'life' or as a verb meaning something like 'is immersed in'. Bernard remarked of the latter interpretation, 'I suppose that's true.' And indeed it is.

ACKNOWLEDGEMENTS

Several people have generously given their time and attention to help me write this book, beginning with my wife Mary. Our daughter Julia, and her husband Phil, both of whom are extremely knowledgeable and highly skilled in using computers, have frequently come to my rescue when I was totally lost in the composition of my book, and were always very generous in giving prompt and effective assistance.

I am particularly grateful to the editorial team at Harvill Secker, especially Geoff Mulligan, who saved me from making a number of mistakes in the text of *Varying Degrees,* and Mikaela Pedlow, who supervised the many revisions and corrections I made in the text in the course of its composition, right up to the time when it went to the printers. Throughout the process I was encouraged by the whole team's enthusiastic support of the book, led by Liz Foley, the Publishing Director of this sector of Penguin Random House in London. I am very grateful to Margaret Drabble for permission to include in it a passage from her book, *The Pattern in the Carpet: A Personal History with Jigsaws,* published by Canongate in 2000.

D.L.

INDEX

207

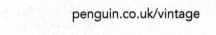
penguin.co.uk/vintage